ALGEBRA

EQUATIONS AND EXPRESSIONS

Walker Maths Essentials: Algebra 4+
1st Edition
Charlotte Walker
Victoria Walker

Designer: Cheryl Smith, Macarn Design
Production controller: Katie McCappin

Any URLs contained in this publication were checked for currency during the production process. Note, however, that the publisher cannot vouch for the ongoing currency of URLs.

Acknowledgements
Cover photo courtesy of Shutterstock.
We wish to thank the Boards of Trustees of Darfield and Riccarton High Schools for allowing us to use materials and ideas developed while teaching. Our thanks also go to all past and present colleagues, especially Kath Wilson, who have generously shared their experience and ideas.

For product information and technology assistance,
in Australia call **1300 790 853**;
in New Zealand call **0800 449 725**

For permission to use material from this text or product, please email
aust.permissions@cengage.com

National Library of New Zealand Cataloguing-in-Publication Data
A catalogue record for this book is available from the National Library of New Zealand.

978 0 17 044741 6

Cengage Learning Australia
Level 7, 80 Dorcas Street
South Melbourne, Victoria Australia 3205

For learning solutions, visit **cengage.co.nz**

Printed in China by 1010 Printing International Limited.
8 25

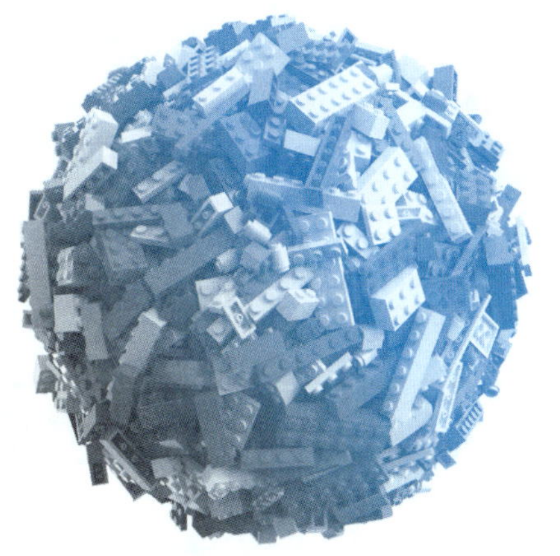

CONTENTS

ISBN: 9780170447416

Glossary

Make your own glossary of key terms:

Term	Definition	Picture/Example
Expression		
Term		
Like terms		
Constant		
Power		
Index (plural: indices)		
Exponent		
Variable		
Coefficient		
Expand		
Factorise		

ISBN: 9780170447416

Term	Definition	Picture/Example
Solve		
Simplify		
Substitute		
Evaluate		
Product		
Sum		
Reciprocal		
Highest Common Factor (HCF)		
Numerator		
Denominator		

ISBN: 9780170447416

Revision

Working with integers

Multiplying and dividing integers:

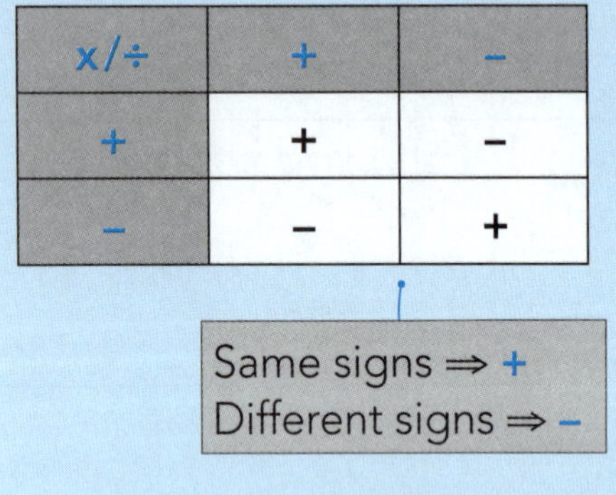

x/÷	+	–
+	+	–
–	–	+

Examples: –2 x +6 = –12

–6 ÷ +3 = –2

Different signs ⇒ –

+6 ÷ +3 = 2

–2 x –6 = 12

Same signs ⇒ +

–2 x –3 x –2 = (–2 x –3) x –2
= (6) x –2
= –12

If there is more than one multiply or divide sign, work from left to right.

Calculate the following.

1 5 x 6 = ______________________ **2** 10 x –2 = ______________________

3 –2 x –4 = ______________________ **4** 15 ÷ 3 = ______________________

5 –6 ÷ 2 = ______________________ **6** –8 ÷ –4 = ______________________

7 –8 x 3 = ______________________ **8** 10 ÷ –5 = ______________________

9 –6 x 2 x 1 = ______________________ **10** –2 x 3 x –2 = ______________________

11 –20 ÷ –5 ÷ 2 = ______________________ **12** –4 x –3 x –2 = ______________________

Adding and subtracting integers:

- Do this on the number line.
- On the number line, start at the position of the first number.
- Then move left (–) or right (+) as appropriate.

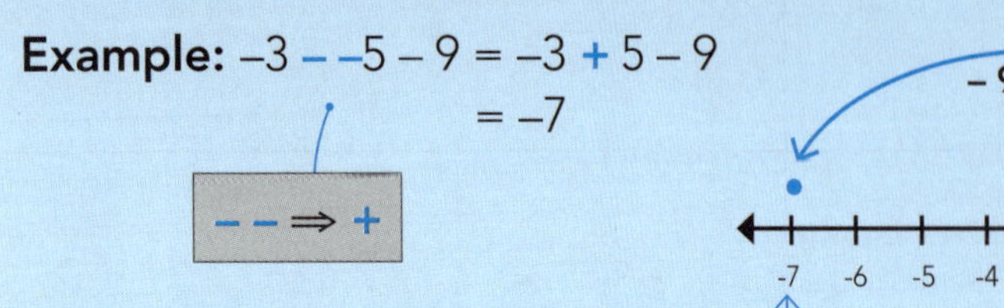

Example: –3 – –5 – 9 = –3 + 5 – 9
= –7

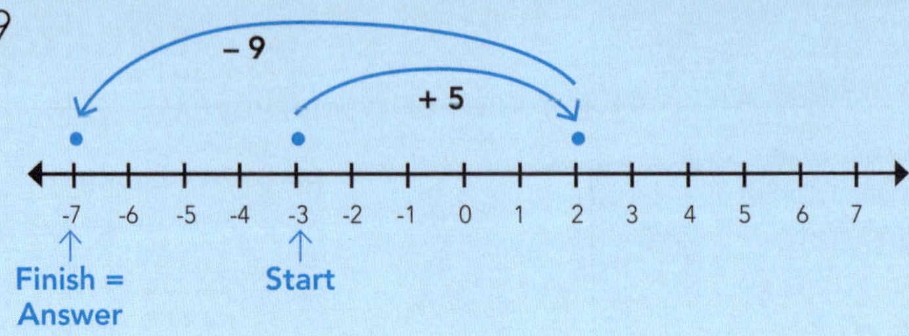

 ISBN: 9780170447416

To help solve these questions, use the number lines and add arrows.

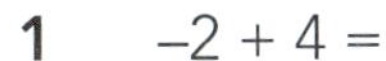

1 $-2 + 4 =$

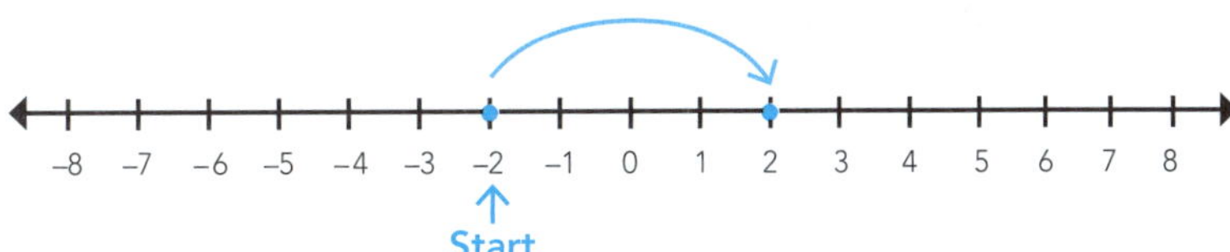

2 $-5 - 2 =$

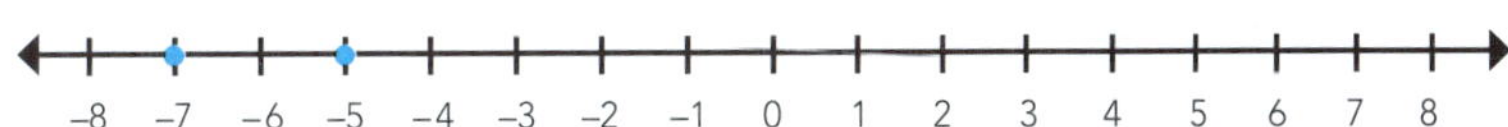

3 $8 - 7 - 5 =$

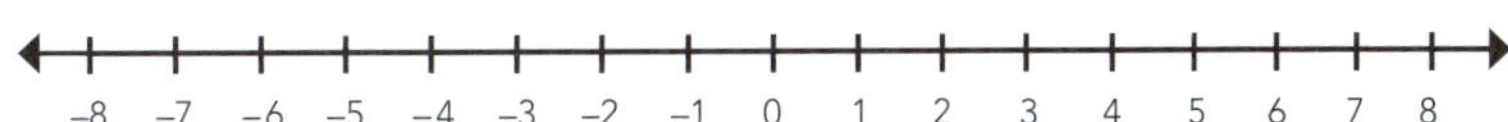

4 $7 - 12 + 3 =$

5 $-2 - 6 + 10 =$

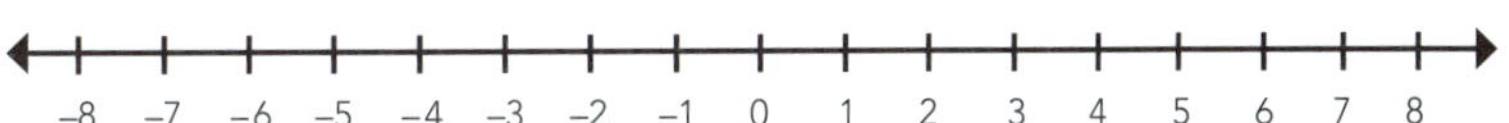

6 $-4 + 11 - 9 + 3 =$

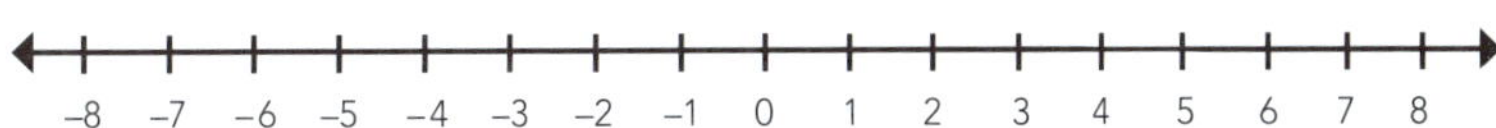

7 $-5 + 10 =$ ____________________

8 $2 - 8 =$ ____________________

9 $-2 + 6 - 5 =$ ____________________

10 $8 + 1 - 9 =$ ____________________

11 $-1 - 4 + 5 =$ ____________________

12 $2 - 8 - 6 + 4 =$ ____________________

13 $-2 + 9 + 3 =$ ____________________

14 $-7 - 2 + 8 =$ ____________________

ISBN: 9780170447416

Order of operations

BEDMAS helps us to remember the order of operations.

Fill in the table below to help remember what order to complete calculations in:

B	
E	
D	
M	
A	
S	

Remember: when there is more than one of these, work from left to right. (D and M; A and S)

Use BEDMAS to calculate the following.

1 $3 + 6 \times 2 =$ ____________

2 $(12 + 7) \times 2 =$ ____________

3 $3 + 2^2 =$ ____________

4 $6 \div 2\,(1 + 2) =$ ____________

5 $5 - 2\,(2 + 3) =$ ____________

6 $3^2 + (2 + 1) =$ ____________

7 $3 + 2 \times 4 - 1 =$ ____________

8 $1 + 4 \times (2 + 3) =$ ____________

9 $10 - 2(4 - 1) =$ ____________

10 $2^2 - 1 \times (8 - 6) =$ ____________

11 $7 - 2 - 3 =$ ____________

12 $4 - 2(3+1) =$ ____________

13 $-6 \div -3 =$ ____________

14 $-8 - 2 =$ ____________

15 $3 + 6 \times -2 =$ ____________

16 $2 \times 4 - 5 =$ ____________

17 $4 + 3^2 =$ ____________

18 $8 \div 4 \times -1 =$ ____________

19 $-4 \times 1 - 1 =$ ____________

20 $2(5 - 2) =$ ____________

21 $-3(8 - 6) =$ ____________

22 $-2(3 - 5) =$ ____________

ISBN: 9780170447416

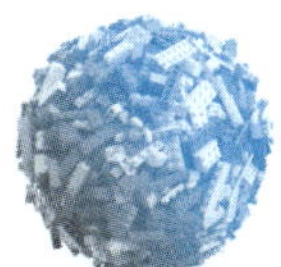

The language of algebra

From words to expressions

Below are two **equivalent** expressions:

A number add on three — This one is written in words.

$N + 3$ — This one is written with symbols. We use this version in algebra.

What are some other terms for these symbols? (Hint: Use the list below if you are stuck.)

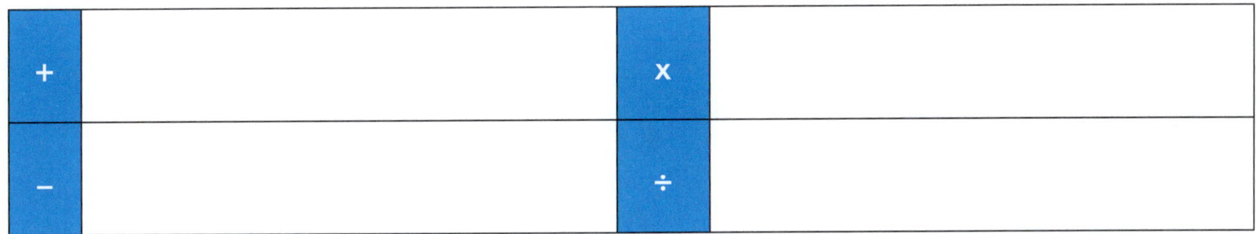

+		x	
–		÷	

multiply, add, subtract, divide, minus, more, less than, plus, take away, times, goes into, lots of, division, sum, decrease, total, split, product

Rewrite these as expressions using symbols.

1 A number plus four

= ***n* +** ______________

2 A number minus two

= ______________

3 Five take away a number

= ______________

4 Two multiplied by a number

= ______________

5 A number divided by nine

= ______________

6 Three less than a number

= ______________

7 Two groups of a number plus one

= ______________

8 A number minus three, then divided by two

= ______________

9 Jeremy has a long piece of liquorice. It is n centimetres long. Jeremy breaks off two centimetres. Write an expression for the length that is left.

= ______________

10 Kathryn has a stack of coins (n). Roger has a stack of coins that is twice as big minus two. Write an expression for Roger's stack. Roger's stack = ______________

ISBN: 9780170447416

Finding the value of a symbol

- The missing numbers in the following are represented by symbols:

1 + ★ = 5 — For this statement to be true, the symbol (★) must take the value **4**.

6 x ☯ = 12 — For this statement to be true, the symbol (☯) must take the value **2**.

10 + ☸ + ☸ = 16 — This time there are two symbols, so together they must equal 6 ∴ each symbol (☸) must take the value **3**.

Write down the value of each symbol for each of the following.

1 3 + ♣ = 7 ♣ = ______ **2** 12 – ✶ = 8 ✶ = ______

3 12 ÷ ♥ = 4 ♥ = ______ **4** ☺ x 3 = 21 ☺ = ______

5 2 + ⌘ + ⌘ = 8 ⌘ = ______ **6** 10 – ✠ – ✠ – ✠ = 7 ✠ = ______

- In algebra, instead of using symbols like those above, we use **letters**.
- The symbols used above can be replaced by letters.
- We call these letters '**variables**' because they can sometimes take different values.

3 + ★ = 9: $3 + s = 9$ — **s** stands for **s**tar (★).

5 x ☯ = 15: $5 \times y = 15$ — **y** stands for **y**in-yang (☯).

10 + ☸ + ☸ = 16: $10 + 2w = 16$ — **w** stands for **w**heel (☸). In this case there are two wheels. Instead of writing **w + w**, we write **2w**.

Write down the value of each variable (letter) for each of the following.

7 $2 + c = 9$ $c =$ ______ **8** $17 - s = 5$ $s =$ ______

9 $22 \div h = 2$ $h =$ ______ **10** $w \times 7 = 21$ $w =$ ______

11 $4 + 2L = 12$ $L =$ ______ **12** $10 - c = 7$ $c =$ ______

 ISBN: 9780170447416

Write down the value of each symbol or letter for each of the following.

1 4 + ♥ = 12 ♥ = ______

2 12 – ⌘ = 8 ⌘ = ______

3 10 ÷ ♣ = 5 ♣ = ______

4 ☺ x 4 = 20 ☺ = ______

5 4 + ✶ + ✶ + ✶ = 10 ✶ = ______

6 12 – ✠ – ✠ = 6 ✠ = ______

7 $3 + h = 8$ h = ______

8 $12 - y = 3$ y = ______

9 $12 \div p = 4$ p = ______

10 $b \times 6 = 24$ b = ______

11 $L + 4 + 1 = 9$ L = ______

12 $13 - c + 1 = 6$ c = ______

13 $4 + g - 2 = 7$ g = ______

14 $2d + 1 = 9$ d = ______

15 Some of the following simplifications are correct and some are incorrect. If the simplification is correct, put a tick in the ✓/✗ column. If it is incorrect, put a cross in the ✓/✗ column, and write the correct solution.

		✓/✗	Correct solution
1	4 + 3 x 2 – 1 = 7 x 1 = 7		
2	14 – ♥ – ♥ = 10 ♥ = 4		
3	3 + 4 x (1 + 5) = 3 + 24 = 27		
4	✠ + ✠ + 3 = 15 ✠ = 5		
5	$5 + c + c = 9$ $c = 2$		
6	4 ÷ 2 + 1 x (5 – 2) = 3 x 3 = 9		

ISBN: 9780170447416

Phrases to expressions

- In algebra we use **operations** along with **variables** and numbers to write **expressions**.
- A **variable** is represented by a **letter of the alphabet**, which may be the initial of what it represents, e.g **d** for **d**istance.

Some tricks:

- We do not write in the times sign between a number and a variable, e.g. $2d$ means $2 \times d$.
- We do not write an exponent for powers of one, e.g. d^1 is written as d.

Some special terms:

Double or twice d	$2 \times d$ or $2d$
Treble or triple d	$3 \times d$ or $3d$
Half of d	$d \div 2$ or $\frac{1}{2}d$ or $\frac{d}{2}$
Quarter of d	$d \div 4$ or $\frac{1}{4}d$ or $\frac{d}{4}$

Note that $2 \times d = d \times 2$, but we write the **number first**: $2d$.

Remember that order doesn't matter when we add, so we can write $b + 10$ or $10 + b$.

Examples:

Phrase	Operation	Variable	Expression
10 more than b	+	b	$b + 10$ or $10 + b$
Five times d	x	d	$5d$
p reduced by 2	–	p	$p - 2$
a fifth of m	÷	m	$m \div 5$ or $\frac{m}{5}$ or $\frac{1}{5}m$

Order is important:
$p - 2 \neq 2 - p$ and $m \div 5 \neq 5 \div m$

 ISBN: 9780170447416

Match the phrases below with the correct expression from the box below:

$f \div 3$	$2e$	$\frac{f}{3}$	$\frac{2}{f}$
$e + f$	$2f$	fe	$e - f$
$f + e$	$e - 3$	$3 - f$	$f \times f$
$\frac{f}{2}$	$f - 2$	$e + 2$	$f - e$

	Phrase	Expression
1	Two times f	
2	e reduced by three	
3	a total of f and e	
4	A number (f) shared between three	
5	Two more than e	
6	Half of f	
7	Subtract f from e	
8	A third of a number (f)	
9	A number (f) that has been subtracted from three	
10	e increased by f	
11	Two divided by f	
12	2 less than f	
13	Twice a number (e)	
14	e less than f	
15	f multiplied by itself	
16	The product of f and e	

ISBN: 9780170447416

Write an expression for these phrases. Use the variable y.

1 A term with ten added to it

2 A variable divided by three

3 Four times a number

4 A number with one subtracted from it

5 Twice a number

6 A number three more than y

7 Eight less than a number

8 Twelve divided by a number

9 Twice a number minus three

10 A term with one subtracted from it and shared between three

Write a phrase for these expressions.

11 $c + 2$

12 $4 - b$

13 $a \div 2$

14 $6 \times y$

15 $12 - g$

16 $\frac{3}{p}$

17 $1 \times y - 4$

18 $f \times 2 - a$

 ISBN: 9780170447416

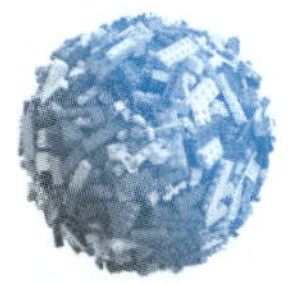

Challenge 1

Solve the following puzzles.

1 If:

▲ + ▲ + ▲ = 30

▲ + ▲ + ■ = 35

■ + ■ + ● = 50

Then:

▲ = ______

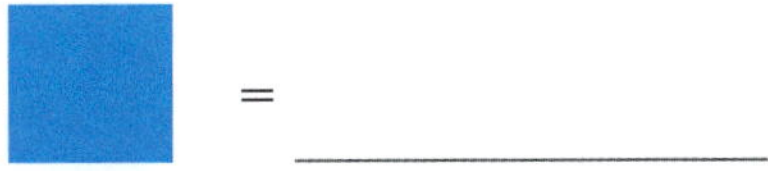

■ = ______

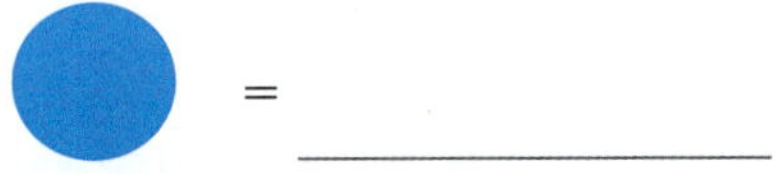

● = ______

2 If:

◇ + ★ = 50

★ + ★ + ★ = 60

♣ + ★ + ◇ = 65

Then:

◇ = ______

★ = ______

♣ = ______

3 If:

⚡ + ⚡ + ⚡ + ⚡ = 36

☾ + ⚡ + ☾ = 29

⚡ + ☾ – ☺ = 4

Then:

⚡ = ______

☾ = ______

☺ = ______

ISBN: 9780170447416

More about variables

- We use **letters** of the alphabet to represent **variables**.
- A **variable** is a quantity that **can change**.

Example:

Grandpa gets twins to do a series of jobs during the school holidays, and pays them different amounts, depending on the job. They share the work and the money equally. They are paid:

$8 for walking the dog: Each twin gets $\$\frac{8}{2} = \$4$

$12 for cleaning the oven: Each twin gets $\$\frac{12}{2} = \$6$

$24 for cleaning the car (inside and out): Each twin gets $\$\frac{24}{2} = \$12$

We call the total amount they were **paid** for each job p, so each twin was paid $\$\frac{p}{2}$.

p is called the **variable** and it represents the amount that Grandpa **pays** for each job. p **changes** depending on how much is paid for each job.

$\frac{p}{2}$ is called an **expression**.

Identify the variable and expression for each of the following.

1 Eve was paid $15 per hour for weeding the garden. She found that the total she was paid each day was given by the expression **Total = 15*h***.

a The variable is ______ and it stands for ________________________________.

b Use the expression to calculate how much she would be paid for three hours' work.

____

2 Edward is having a birthday party. He has three cousins who will be there, as well as some friends. The number at his party (counting himself) is given by the expression **Total = *f* + 4**.

a The variable is ______ and it stands for ________________________________.

b Use the expression to calculate how many will be at his party if he asks five friends.

____

3 Marvin is planting bean seeds. He needs three stakes for his first row, and one more for each extra row. He worked out that the number of stakes needed was given by the expression **Total = 2*r* + 1**.

a The variable is ______ and it stands for ________________________________.

b Use the expression to calculate how many stakes he would need for five rows.

____

ISBN: 9780170447416

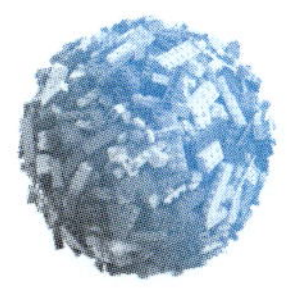

Simplifying expressions

Multiplying

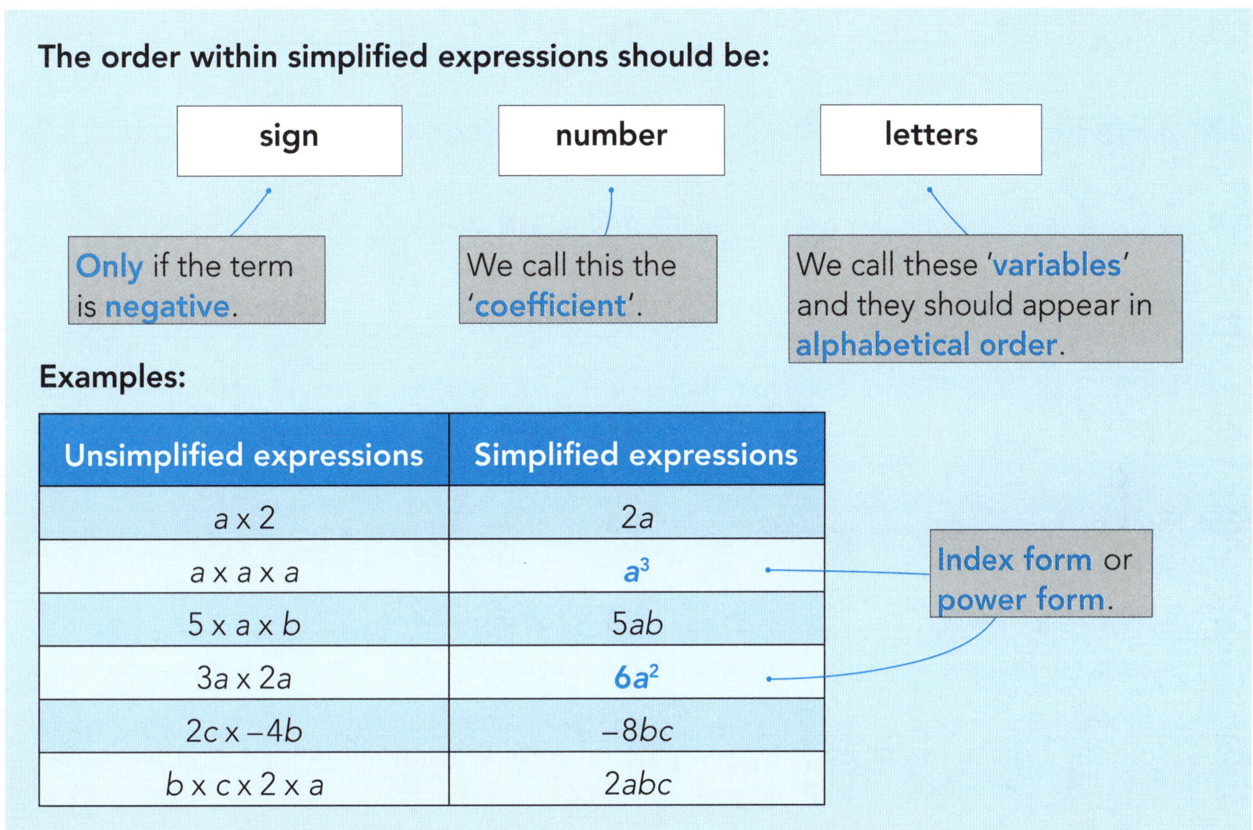

The order within simplified expressions should be:

sign	number	letters
Only if the term is **negative**.	We call this the '**coefficient**'.	We call these '**variables**' and they should appear in **alphabetical order**.

Examples:

Unsimplified expressions	Simplified expressions
$a \times 2$	$2a$
$a \times a \times a$	a^3
$5 \times a \times b$	$5ab$
$3a \times 2a$	$6a^2$
$2c \times -4b$	$-8bc$
$b \times c \times 2 \times a$	$2abc$

Index form or **power form**.

Circle/highlight the correct/best simplified answer for each of the following.

1	$3 \times a$	$a3$	$3a$
		$3 + a$	a^3
2	$p \times p \times p$	p^3	$p + 3$
		$p3$	$3p$
3	$2 \times a \times f$	$fa2$	af^2
		$2af$	$2 + af$
4	$3g \times 2$	$g5$	$6g$
		$5g$	$g6$
5	$4a \times 2b$	ab^8	$8ab$
		$ba6$	$6ab$
6	$4b \times 3b$	$7b$	$12b$
		$7b^2$	$12b^2$
7	$y \times y$	${}^2y$	$2y$
		$y2$	y^2
8	$3e \times 2f \times 1g$	$5efg$	$6ef$
		$6efg$	$5gfe$
9	$4 \times -g$	$4g$	$-4g$
		$g4$	$-g4$
10	$2a \times -3$	$-6a$	$-5a$
		$6a$	$5a$

ISBN: 9780170447416

Simplify the following expressions.

11 $a \times a =$ ____________ **12** $b \times f \times g =$ ____________

13 $8 \times b =$ ____________ **14** $2e \times 3c =$ ____________

15 $-2 \times a =$ ____________ **16** $f \times s \times 4 =$ ____________

17 $3 \times f \times 5 =$ ____________ **18** $-3 \times -2 \times g =$ ____________

19 $2 \times p \times -4 =$ ____________ **20** $-3p \times -7q =$ ____________

21 $-4b \times -5 =$ ____________ **22** $5m \times m =$ ____________

23 $f \times f \times f =$ ____________ **24** $-2g \times -1 =$ ____________

25 $3p \times 6p =$ ____________ **26** $-8f \times -2f =$ ____________

27 $-2d \times -1 \times -4 =$ ____________ **28** $2 \times -5p \times -4 =$ ____________

29 Join the dots to match each term on the left with the simplified term on the right.

$6 \times a \times b$ •	• $-6ab$
$1 \times b \times a \times -6$ •	• $6b^3$
$-3 \times 2 \times b$ •	• $6a^2$
$2 \times a \times 3 \times a$ •	• $-6b^2$
$a \times -2 \times -3$ •	• $6b^2$
$-2a \times -3 \times -1$ •	• $6ab$
$a \times -6 \times b \times b$ •	• $-6ab^2$
$b \times 6 \times -1 \times b$ •	• $6b$
$b \times b \times b \times 6$ •	• $6a$
$2 \times b \times 3$ •	• $-6b$
	• $-6a$

Which term is left over? ____________

 ISBN: 9780170447416

Dividing

- 'x divided by y' can be written as either $x \div y$ or $\frac{x}{y}$.
- Don't forget that $\frac{x}{x} = 1$, so you can 'cancel'.

Example: $\frac{12b}{3} = \frac{4b}{1} \times \frac{3}{3}$

$= 4b$

Remember:

1 $\frac{\text{anything}}{1}$ = itself e.g. $\frac{3}{1} = 3$

2 $\frac{\text{anything}}{\text{itself}} = 1$ e.g. $\frac{3}{3} = 1$

More examples:

Unsimplified expressions	Simplified expressions
$a \div 4$	$\frac{a}{4}$ or $\frac{1}{4}a$
$6 \div a$	$\frac{6}{a}$
$\frac{2a}{4}$	$\frac{a}{2}$ or $\frac{1}{2}a$
$\frac{9b}{3a}$	$\frac{3b}{a}$

Circle/highlight the correct/best expression for each of the following.

	Expression		
1	$b \div 2$	$2b$	b^2
		$\frac{b}{2}$	$\frac{2}{b}$
3	$a \div 5$	$\frac{1}{5}a$	$\frac{1}{5a}$
		$5a$	a^5
5	$\frac{4f}{8}$	$\frac{2f}{4}$	$\frac{f}{2}$
		$\frac{2}{4f}$	$\frac{1}{2f}$

	Expression		
2	$3 \div g$	$\frac{g}{3}$	$\frac{3}{g}$
		$3g$	$g3$
4	$\frac{6d}{2}$	$\frac{d}{3}$	$\frac{1}{3}d$
		$d3$	$3d$
6	$\frac{12}{6b}$	$\frac{2}{b}$	$\frac{b}{2}$
		$2b$	$\frac{6}{3b}$

ISBN: 9780170447416

Simplify the following expressions.

7 $2y \div 4 =$ ______________________

8 $16d \div 8 =$ ______________________

9 $20 \div 5e =$ ______________________

10 $10b \div 5a =$ ______________________

11 $12b \div 4f =$ ______________________

12 $\frac{4g}{8} =$ ______________________

13 $\frac{3}{9p} =$ ______________________

14 $\frac{15h}{5r} =$ ______________________

15 $\frac{18m}{6} =$ ______________________

16 $\frac{7}{21a} =$ ______________________

17 $\frac{3b}{21a} =$ ______________________

18 $\frac{18}{9w} =$ ______________________

19 $24z \div 6v =$ ______________________

20 $\frac{-4b}{2} =$ ______________________

21 $\frac{-18p}{-9} =$ ______________________

22 $5b \div 2 =$ ______________________

23 Join the dots to match each term on the left with the simplified term on the right.

$4f \div 2$ •	• $-\frac{f}{2}$
$\frac{-4}{2f}$ •	• $\frac{f}{2}$
$\frac{8}{4f}$ •	• $-\frac{2}{f}$
$2f \div 4$ •	• $-2f$
$\frac{16f}{-8}$ •	• $\frac{2}{f}$
$-8f \div 16$ •	• $2f$

ISBN: 9780170447416

Putting it together

Use the simplified terms in the boxes as answers to the questions below. You should use each answer only once.

$5p$	$\frac{p}{2}$	$2mp$	$\frac{2}{m}$
$2p$	p^2	$6p$	$3mp$
$6mp$	$3p$	$2p^2$	$-6p$
$\frac{1}{6p}$	$2m$	$\frac{5}{p}$	$\frac{p}{5}$

Simplify each of the following.

1 $p \times p =$ ________________

2 $\frac{4p}{2} =$ ________________

3 $\frac{2p}{4} =$ ________________

4 $2p \times 3 =$ ________________

5 $\frac{2}{12p} =$ ________________

6 $2 \times p \times m =$ ________________

7 $3 \times m \times 2 \times p =$ ________________

8 $\frac{8}{4m} =$ ________________

9 $6p \div 2 =$ ________________

10 $2 \times -3p =$ ________________

11 $p \times 3m =$ ________________

12 $5 \div p =$ ________________

13 $\frac{25p}{5} =$ ________________

14 $p \times 2p =$ ________________

15 $2p \div 10 =$ ________________

16 $\frac{6m}{3} =$ ________________

ISBN: 9780170447416

Like terms

- Terms can only be added or subtracted if they are '**like**' terms.
- 'Like' terms must have exactly the **same variables**, and each variable must be raised to exactly the **same power**.
- Order does not matter.
- The sign does not matter.

Examples: The following **are** like terms: ab, $2ab$, ba, $-ab$.
The following are **not** like terms:
ab and $ba\mathbf{c}$ — Includes a '**c**' term.
ab^2 and ab — First term has b^2, second term does not.

State whether each of the following pairs are like terms or unlike terms.

1 x and y ________
2 x and $2x$ ________
3 $2xy$ and $3yx$ ________
4 $2x$ and $3y$ ________
5 x and $100x$ ________
6 x and $-2x$ ________
7 xy and xy ________
8 $3y$ and x ________
9 xy and yx ________
10 $2xy$ and $4x$ ________
11 $2x$ and x^2 ________
12 7 and 1 ________
13 xy and xy^2 ________
14 b and $2b$ ________
15 bc and cb ________
16 bc^2 and bc ________
17 gp and gp^2 ________
18 x^2y and yx^2 ________
19 $10xy$ and $3xy$ ________
20 -8 and 2 ________

Write three like terms for these.

1 a ________________
2 $4g$ ________________
3 y^2 ________________
4 $5hd$ ________________
5 7 ________________
6 $-6p$ ________________
7 $-2x^2$ ________________
8 xyz ________________
9 $0.5m$ ________________
10 $-ew$ ________________

ISBN: 9780170447416

Adding and subtracting

- When adding or subtracting, you can **combine only like terms**.
- Only the ones with **exactly** the same variables and powers can be combined.

Hint: It is helpful to circle, underline or highlight terms that are 'like' each other with the same shape or colour.

Examples: Simplify these.

1 $3p + 2r + p = 4p + 2r$

$3p$ and $+p$ are like terms, so they can be combined → $4p$.
$2r$ has no other like terms so remains the same.

2 $5a + 2b - a = 4a + 2b$

$5a$ and $-a$ are like terms, so they can be combined → $4a$.

Remember, the sign before the term belongs to it.

A Fill the boxes with letters and/or numbers in order to complete a correct simplification.

1 $a + a =$ ☐

2 $p + p + p =$ ☐

3 $2y + 3y =$ ☐

4 $4f - f =$ ☐

5 $a + a + 3a =$ ☐

6 $6b + 3b - b =$ ☐

7 $3g - 5g + 4g =$ ☐

8 $2a + 3b + a + 4b = 3a +$ ☐

9 $5f + 3p + p + 2f =$ ☐ $+ 4p$

10 $6y + 10 - y + 2 = 5y +$ ☐

11 $8z + 3y - z - 2y = 7z +$ ☐

12 $3p + w + 2p + p =$ ☐ $+ w$

13 $5d + 7e - e - 4d = d +$ ☐

14 $6b + 4c - b + 2c =$ ☐ $+ 6c$

15 $3y + 5z - 5y + 3z =$ ☐ $+ 8z$

16 $2a + b + 2b + 2c + a =$ ☐ $+$ ☐ $+ 2c$

17 $5a^2 + a + a^2 = 6a^2 +$ ☐

18 $3y^2 + 8y + y^2 - 6y =$ ☐ $+ 2y$

ISBN: 9780170447416

B Circle/highlight the correct/best simplified answer for each of the following.

1	$p + p =$	p^2	$p2$
		$2p$	^2p
3	$8a - 2a$	$6a$	$6a^2$
		$6aa$	$a6$
5	$3a + a + a$	$3aaa$	$a5$
		$3a$	$5a$
7	$5a + 2b - 1a$	$6ab$	$7ab - a$
		$4a + 2b$	$6a + 2b$
9	$2b - 2b$	b	1
		$4b$	0
11	$2a + 4a + b + 3b$	$7a + 3b$	$6a + 3b$
		$6a + 4b$	$7a - 3b$

2	$2a + 6a =$	$12a$	$8a$
		a^{12}	a^8
4	$5b + c + 2b$	$7b + c$	$7b - c$
		$3b + c$	$7b^2 + c$
6	$f + f + f - f$	$3f$	$2f$
		f^2	$1f$
8	$4y - y + y$	$5y$	y
		$4y$	$3y$
10	$3a + 2b + a + b$	$3a - 4b$	$4a + 3b$
		$4a - 3b$	$3a + 4b$
12	$5a + 5b - a - 3b$	$4a + 2b$	$4a + 3b$
		$4b + 2a$	$4a - 2b$

C Simplify these by adding or subtracting like terms.

1 $a + a + a =$ ______________

2 $x + 2x + 3x =$ ______________

3 $8a - 2a + a =$ ______________

4 $7y + y - 2y + y =$ ______________

5 $3a + b + a =$ ______________

6 $y + y + 3 =$ ______________

7 $2y + 4x - x =$ ______________

8 $4a + b + a =$ ______________

9 $5x + 4y - 2x - y =$ ______________

10 $9p + 4q - 6p - 2q =$ ______________

11 $8a - a + b + 4b =$ ______________

12 $7y + 7 - 3x - 2 =$ ______________

13 $4f + 3g - 2f - g + e =$ ______________

14 $5x - 4y + x + y =$ ______________

15 $x^2 + x + x =$ ______________

16 $p^2 - p + p^2 - p =$ ______________

 ISBN: 9780170447416

Mixing it up

Highlight the boxes which contain an expression that is equivalent to the central expression.

$7a + 2b - 2a - 2b$	$\frac{2}{12a}$	$a \times 6$	$8a - a + a$
$12a - 6a$			$6 \times a \times 1$
	$6a$		
$\frac{12a}{2}$			$8a - 2$
$a + 3a - a + 4a$	$3a \times 2$	$\frac{12a}{6}$	$24a \div 4a$

Find the errors

Some of the following statements are correct and some are incorrect. If the statement is correct, put a tick in the ✓/✗ column. If it is incorrect, put a cross in the ✓/✗ column, and write the correct solution.

		✓/✗	Correct solution
1	$2t \times 5t = 10t$		
2	$12 \div 3m = 4m$		
3	$15f + 2g - 10f - g = 5f + g$		
4	$\frac{12pq}{4} = 3pq$		
5	$6a + a - 2 - a + 7 = 6a + 9$		
6	$p \times p \times 3 = 3p$		
7	$a + a^2 + a = a^2 + 2a$		

ISBN: 9780170447416

Powers

The words **power**, **exponent** and **index** all mean the same thing.

$5a^4$ — coefficient: 5; base: a; power, exponent, index: 4

You need to know that:

- a^4 means **a x a x a x a**
- a^1 is the same as **a**
- $a^0 = 1$ — This is important but often forgotten. It only works as long as $a \neq 0$.

Multiplying powers

When multiplying, we **add** the indices: $a^n \times a^m = a^{n+m}$

Examples:

1 $a^3 \times a^2 = a \times a \times a \times a \times a$
$= a^5$ ($3 + 2 = 5$)

If you are not sure, expand each term.

2 $2ab \times 7ab^2 = 2 \times a \times b \times 7 \times a \times b \times b$
$= 14a^2b^3$

3 $3a^4 \times 5a^9 = 15a^{13}$ — It helps to deal with the **coefficients** first.

Circle/highlight the correct/best simplified answer for each of the following.

1	$a \times a$	$2a$	a^2
		$a2$	a^2a
2	$b^2 \times b^3$	b^5	b^6
		$6b$	$5b$
3	$y \times y^2$	y^2	$3y$
		$2y$	y^3
4	$2f \times f^2$	$2f^2$	f^3
		$2f^3$	$3f^3$
5	$3p \times 2p$	$5p^2$	$6p^2$
		$6p$	$2p^6$
6	$2d^2 \times 4d^3$	$6d^5$	$8d^5$
		$8d^6$	$6d^6$
7	$a \times a^3$	a^4	a^3
		$2a^3$	$2a^4$
8	$2b \times a$	$2ab$	ab^2
		ba	$2ba^2$

ISBN: 9780170447416

Simplify these.

9 $b \times b \times b =$ ____________

10 $a^2 \times a =$ ____________

11 $y^3 \times y^3 =$ ____________

12 $m^2 \times m \times m^3 =$ ____________

13 $g^2 \times 2g =$ ____________

14 $3b^4 \times 4b =$ ____________

15 $6a^2 \times 2a =$ ____________

16 $3p^4 \times 7p^2 =$ ____________

17 $3h^3 \times 5h^2 =$ ____________

18 $b^2 \times b \times b^4 =$ ____________

19 $4y^3 \times 5y^3 =$ ____________

20 $h^3 \times h^2 \times h^2 =$ ____________

21 $3a \times a^2 \times 2a =$ ____________

22 $ab \times ab =$ ____________

23 $4fg \times 6fg =$ ____________

24 $2yz \times yz =$ ____________

25 $y^2z \times yz^2 =$ ____________

26 $2ab^2 \times 3a^4b =$ ____________

27 Join the dots to match each term on the left with the simplified term on the right.

$a \times a \times a$ •	• $3a$
$2a \times 3a$ •	• $6a^2$
$a^2 \times 1$ •	• $2a^3$
$a \times a \times a \times 3$ •	• a^2
$2a \times a^2$ •	• a^3
$3a \times a$ •	• $3a^2$
$1 \times 3a$ •	• $2a$
	• $3a^3$

Which term is left over? ________________

ISBN: 9780170447416

Dividing powers

When dividing, we **subtract** the indices: $a^n \div a^m = a^{n-m}$

Examples: 1 $a^5 \div a^2 = \frac{a \times a \times a \times a \times a}{a \times a}$

$= a^3$

5 – 2 = 3

Once again, if you are not sure, expand each term.

2 $\frac{12a^6}{4a^2} = \frac{4 \times 3 \times a \times a \times a \times a \times a \times a}{4 \times a \times a}$

$= 3a^4$

Deal with the **coefficients** first.

3 $\frac{a^3b^2}{a^2b} = \frac{a \times a \times a \times b \times b}{a \times a \times b}$

$= \frac{ab}{1} = ab$

If your denominator is 1, then you don't need to write it.

Circle/highlight the correct/best simplified answer for each of the following.

1	$b^5 \div b^2$	b^{10}	$2b^7$
		$2b^3$	b^3
2	$\frac{f^4}{f}$	f^4	$4f$
		f^3	$3f$
3	$\frac{14a^{10}}{2a^2}$	$7a^8$	$7a^{12}$
		$7a$	$8a^7$
4	$\frac{2b^3}{6}$	$\frac{b^3}{3}$	$3b^3$
		$\frac{b^2}{3}$	$\frac{b^3}{6}$
5	$\frac{a^4b^5}{a^2b^3}$	a^2b^2	a^8b^2
		$\frac{a^2}{b^2}$	$\frac{b^2}{a^2}$
6	$\frac{6f^3g^6}{2fg^2}$	$4f^2g^4$	$4f^3g^3$
		$3f^2g^4$	$3f^3g^3$

 ISBN: 9780170447416

Simplify these.

7 $\frac{b^6}{b^2} =$ ____________

8 $c^5 \div c^2 =$ ____________

9 $\frac{z^3}{z} =$ ____________

10 $y^6 \div y =$ ____________

11 $\frac{a^7}{a^3} =$ ____________

12 $g^6 \div g^5 =$ ____________

13 $\frac{6p^2}{2p} =$ ____________

14 $\frac{10y^4}{5y^3} =$ ____________

15 $\frac{16b^3}{4b^2} =$ ____________

16 $\frac{8a^7}{2a^4} =$ ____________

17 $\frac{2g^3}{6g} =$ ____________

18 $\frac{y^3 z^4}{y^2 z^2} =$ ____________

Find the errors

Some of the following statements are correct and some are incorrect. If the statement is correct, put a tick in the ✓/✗ column. If it is incorrect, put a cross in the ✓/✗ column, and write the correct solution.

		✓/✗	Correct solution
1	$y^4 \div y^2 = y^6$		
2	$\frac{a^3}{a} = a^3$		
3	$b^5 \div b^2 = b^3$		
4	$\frac{8z^2}{2z} = 4z$		
5	$\frac{10p^2}{5p^2} = 2p^4$		
6	$\frac{x^2 y^4}{xy^2} = xy$		

ISBN: 9780170447416

Powers of powers

When finding a power of a power, we **multiply** the indices: **$(a^n)^m = a^{n \times m}$**

Examples: **1** $(a^5)^2 = (a \times a \times a \times a \times a) \times (a \times a \times a \times a \times a)$
$= a^{10}$

$5 \times 2 = 10$

Once again, if you are not sure, expand each term.

2 $(2a^3)^3 = (2 \times a \times a \times a) \times (2 \times a \times a \times a) \times (2 \times a \times a \times a)$
$= 8a^9$

Deal with the **coefficient** first: $2^3 = 8$.

Circle/highlight the correct/best simplified answer for each of the following.

1	$(a^3)^2$	a^5	a^6
		a^2	a^7
2	$(b^4)^3$	b^7	$2b^{12}$
		b^{12}	$2b^7$
3	$(2f)^2$	$2f^2$	$2f^4$
		$4f^2$	$4f^4$
4	$(2y^4)^2$	$4y^6$	$2y^8$
		$4y^8$	$2y^6$
5	$(5g^3)^2$	$25g^6$	$25g^5$
		$10g^6$	$10g^5$
6	$(y^3z^2)^2$	y^6z^4	y^5z^4
		y^4z^5	y^4z^6
7	$(3xy)^2$	$3x^2y^2$	$9x^2y^2$
		$9xy^2$	$3xy^2$
8	$(4ab^2)^2$	$4ab^4$	$16ab^4$
		$16a^2b^4$	$4a^2b^4$
9	$(6g^3h)^2$	$36g^3h^2$	$36g^6h^2$
		$36g^5h^2$	$36g^6h$
10	$(2y^3z^2)^2$	$4y^5z^4$	$2y^6z^4$
		$4y^6z^4$	$2y^5z^4$

ISBN: 9780170447416

Simplify these.

11 $(b^5)^3 =$ ______________________

12 $(a^8)^4 =$ ______________________

13 $(2x^3)^2 =$ ______________________

14 $(3y^4)^3 =$ ______________________

15 $(a^3b)^2 =$ ______________________

16 $5(2p^3)^2 =$ ______________________

17 $(x^3y)^4 =$ ______________________

18 $(2ab)^2 =$ ______________________

19 $(4d^5e^{10})^2 =$ ______________________

20 $(5p^6q)^3 =$ ______________________

21 $(3ab^2)^2 =$ ______________________

22 $(2p^2q^4)^3 =$ ______________________

23 Join the dots to match each term on the left with the simplified term on the right.

$(2a)^2$ •	• $16a^4$
$(2a^2)^2$ •	• a^2
$(2a^2)^4$ •	• $4a^4$
$(4a^2)^2$ •	• a^4
$(1a)^2$ •	• $16a^2$
$(4a)^2$ •	• $4a^2$
$(1a)^4$ •	• $16a^6$
	• $16a^8$

Which term is left over? ______________________

ISBN: 9780170447416

Mixing it up

A Simplify the following.

1 $a^8 \div a^2 =$ __________

2 $a^8 \times a^2 =$ __________

3 $(b^4)^3 =$ __________

4 $\frac{g^5}{g^3} =$ __________

5 $\frac{a^3}{a} =$ __________

6 $(d^5)^3 =$ __________

7 $e \times e^4 =$ __________

8 $(3f)^2 =$ __________

9 $10y^2 \div 5 =$ __________

10 $\frac{9a^4}{3a} =$ __________

11 $4k^3 \times 2k =$ __________

12 $(4p^3)^2 =$ __________

B Highlight the boxes which contain an expression that is equivalent to the central expression.

Central expression: $4a^2$

$(4a)^2$	$16a \div 4a$	$4a \times a$	$(4a)^2 \div 4$
$3a^2 \div 12$			$2 \times a \times 2 \times a$
$\frac{8a^2}{2a}$			$(2a^2)^2$
$2a^2 \times 2$	$(2a)^2$	$\frac{24a^3}{6a}$	$a^2 \times 4a$

 ISBN: 9780170447416

Find the errors

Some of the following statements are correct and some are incorrect. If the statement is correct, put a tick in the ✓/✗ column. If it is incorrect, put a cross in the ✓/✗ column, explain the error, and write the correct solution.

		✓/✗	Explanation	Correct solution
1	$p + p + p + p = 5p$			
2	$2f^2 + f = 2f^3$			
3	$h^3 \times h^2 = h^5$			
4	$(a^2)^3 = a^5$			
5	$10y^2 \div 5y = 2y^3$			
6	$3z^3 \times 2z^2 = 6z^6$			
7	$\frac{6p^2}{2p} = 3p$			
8	$(5b)^3 = 15b^3$			
9	$2s^2 + 3s^2 = 5s^2$			
10	$xy^2 = y^2x$			

ISBN: 9780170447416

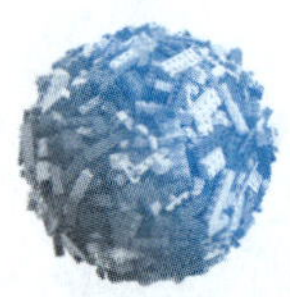

Challenge 2

1 Highlight the boxes which contain an expression that is equivalent to the central expression.

$3a \times 4$	$\frac{12a^2}{a}$	$3a^2 \times 4a$	$3a^2 + a + 8a^2$
$20a^2 + 3 - 8a^2 - 3$			$12a^2 \div a^4$
	$12a^2$		
$-2a \times -6a$			$-12a \times -a$
$a + a \times 12$	$(4a)^3$	$\frac{24a^6}{2a^4}$	$\frac{12a^3b}{ab}$

2 Solve the following puzzles.

If:

♥ x ♥ = 16

♥ x ☺ x ☺ = 36

♥ x ☺ x ✚ = 72

♥ x ☺ + ♣ = 20

☾ – ✚ x ☺ = 12

Then:

♥ = ______________

☺ = ______________

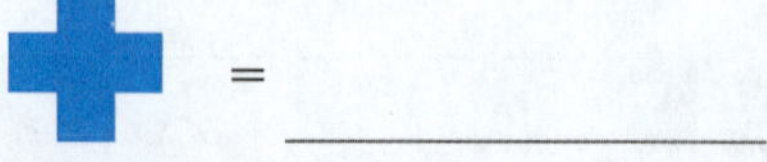

✚ = ______________

♣ = ______________

☾ = ______________

 ISBN: 9780170447416

Brackets

Expanding

- In algebra, '**expand**' means **multiply** out all the **brackets**.
- After expanding you are expected to **collect the like terms** in order to simply the expression.

If there is **no sign** between a term and a bracket, it is understood that you should **multiply**.

$2(a + 3) = 2 \times a + 2 \times 3$
$= 2a + 6$

Examples: Expand the following.

1 $4(b + 3) = 4b + 12$ — $4 \times b + 4 \times 3$

2 $4(b - 2) = 4b - 8$ — $4 \times b + - 4 \times 2$

3 $3(2b + 5) = 6b + 15$ — $3 \times 2b + 3 \times 5$

4 $a(b + c) = ab + ac$ — $a \times b + a \times c$

Remember, a positive of a negative is a **negative**.

A Fill the boxes with letters and/or numbers in order to complete a correct expansion.

1	$2(x + 5) = \square + 10$	**2**	$3(x + 2) = 3x + \square$
3	$5(y + 4) = \square + 20$	**4**	$6(a + b) = 6a + \square$
5	$2(x - 3) = \square - 6$	**6**	$5(c - 3) = 5c - \square$
7	$3(y - 4) = \square - 12$	**8**	$2(p - g) = 2p - \square$
9	$2(3 + x) = 6 + \square$	**10**	$5(3 - y) = 15 - \square$
11	$2(5a + 2) = \square + 4$	**12**	$4(2x - 3) = 8x - \square$

ISBN: 9780170447416

B Circle/highlight the correct expanded answer for each of the following.

1	$2(a+b)$	$2a+b$ $2a+2b$ $a+2b$ $2ab$	**2**	$3(x+2)$	$3x+6$ $x+6$ $3x-6$ $3x+5$
3	$5(y+2)$	$5y+7$ $y+10$ $5y+10$ $y+7$	**4**	$4(a-2)$	$4a-2$ $a+8$ $4a-8$ $a-8$
5	$2(x-y)$	$2x+2y$ $2x-y$ $2x-2y$ $-2x-2y$	**6**	$x(y+z)$	$xy+z$ $y+xz$ $xy-xz$ $xy+xz$
7	$2(3x+4)$	$6x+8$ $3x+8$ $6x+4$ $3x-8$	**8**	$x(x+3)$	x^2+3x $2x+3x$ x^2+3 $x+3x$

C Expand the following.

1 $2(x+4) =$ ____________________ **2** $3(x+4) =$ ____________________

3 $5(y-2) =$ ____________________ **4** $6(x-4) =$ ____________________

5 $2(a+c) =$ ____________________ **6** $3(x-y) =$ ____________________

7 $2(2x+3) =$ ____________________ **8** $3(2b-2) =$ ____________________

9 $4(3+y) =$ ____________________ **10** $2(5-y) =$ ____________________

11 $2(x+y+z) =$ ____________________ **12** $a(a+5) =$ ____________________

13 $2(3a+b+c) =$ ____________________ **14** $6a(2+b) =$ ____________________

ISBN: 9780170447416

Factorising

- Factors are terms that are **multiplied** together (rather than added or subtracted), e.g. 2 and 3 are factors of 6 because 2 **x** 3 = 6.
- In algebra, factorising is the '**undoing**' **of expanding**.
- Expressions with brackets are usually in **factorised form**.

Examples:

Expand →

Factorised form	Unfactorised (expanded) form
$2(x + 4)$	$2x + 8$
$3(a + b)$	$3a + 3b$
$3(2 + y)$	$6 + 3y$
$x(x - 5)$	$x^2 - 5x$

← Factorise

Remember, if there is **no sign** between a term and a bracket, it is understood that you should **multiply**.

Finding the biggest factor:

- When factorising, you must factorise **completely**. There must be **no common factor** for the terms inside the brackets.
- You need to ask yourself: '**What is the biggest term (highest common factor or HCF) that will divide into every term?**'
- Do not use fractions or decimals when factorising.

Examples:

Terms	Common factors	Highest common factor (HCF)
6 and 12	1, 2, 3, 6	6
$24p$ and $18p$	$1, 2, 3, 6, p, 2p, 3p, 6p$	$6p$
$15p^2q$ and $6pq^2$	$1, 3, p, q, 3p, 3q, pq, 3pq$	$3pq$

A Write the factors of these numbers, highlight the common ones and identify the largest.

1 Factors of 12: ____________________
Factors of 20: ____________________
→ The highest common factor of 12 and 20 is: ____________________

2 Factors of 18: ____________________
Factors of 30: ____________________
→ The highest common factor of 18 and 30 is: ____________________

3 Factors of 24: ____________________
Factors of 36: ____________________
→ The highest common factor of 24 and 36 is: ____________________

ISBN: 9780170447416

B List the common factors of these terms, then highlight the highest.

1 4, 8 ______________ **2** 2, 10 ______________

3 12, 16 ______________ **4** 15, 20 ______________

5 16, 24 ______________ **6** 6, 8 ______________

7 $2x$, 6 ______________ **8** $3y$, 12 ______________

9 $15y$, 16 ______________ **10** ab, ac ______________

11 $3x$, $8x$ ______________ **12** $2y$, $16y$ ______________

Hints: 1 If you are asked to factorise, check your answer by expanding.
2 If you are asked to expand, check your answer by factorising.

C Fill the boxes with letters and/or numbers in order to complete a correct factorisation.

1 $2x + 2 = 2(\square + 1)$ **2** $4x + 4 = 4(x + \square)$

3 $5x + 10 = 5(x + \square)$ **4** $4x - 20 = 4(x - \square)$

5 $3x - 9 = 3(\square - 3)$ **6** $6 + 2x = 2(\square + x)$

7 $4y + 12 = 4(y + \square)$ **8** $8x - 16 = 8(\square - 2)$

9 $xy + xz = x(\square + z)$ **10** $x^2 + 3x = x(x + \square)$

D Fill the boxes with letters and/or numbers in order to complete a correct factorisation.

1 $3x + 12 = \square(x + 4)$ **2** $2x + 10 = \square(x + 5)$

3 $5x - 15 = \square(x - 3)$ **4** $4x + 16 = \square(x + 4)$

5 $4x - 8 = \square(x - 2)$ **6** $8x - 6 = \square(4x - 3)$

7 $12x + 10 = \square(6x + 5)$ **8** $18x - 6 = \square(3x - 1)$

9 $ab + ac = \square(b + c)$ **10** $xy - xz = \square(y - z)$

11 $9 + 3x = \square(3 + x)$ **12** $5 + 10x = \square(1 + 2x)$

ISBN: 9780170447416

E Write the contents of each bracket in order to complete a correct factorisation.

1 $2x + 10 = 2($ ________ $)$ **2** $4x + 8 = 4($ ________ $)$

3 $3x + 15 = 3($ ________ $)$ **4** $5x - 10 = 5($ ________ $)$

5 $4x - 12 = 4($ ________ $)$ **6** $22x - 33 = 11($ ________ $)$

7 $20 + 10x = 10($ ________ $)$ **8** $16 - 4x = 4($ ________ $)$

9 $gf + gh = g($ ________ $)$ **10** $bc - be = b($ ________ $)$

11 $18 - 9x = 9($ ________ $)$ **12** $x^2 + 10x = x($ ________ $)$

F Circle/highlight the correct factorised answer for each of the following.

1	$2x + 4$	$1(2x + 4)$ $2(x + 4)$ $2(x + 2)$ $2(1x + 4)$
3	$5x + 10$	$5(2x + 2)$ $10(x + 1)$ $x(5 + 2)$ $5(x + 10)$
5	$3x - 12$	$4(x - 3)$ $3(x - 4)$ $3(x + 4)$ $x(3 - 12)$
7	$12 + 4y$	$1(12 + 4y)$ $2(6 + 2y)$ $4(3 + y)$ $4(3 - 4y)$
9	$6x - 6y$	$6(x + y)$ $-6(x - y)$ $-6(x + y)$ $6(x - y)$

2	$6x + 6y$	$2(3x + 3y)$ $3(2x + 2y)$ $6(x + y)$ $6(x - y)$
4	$2x - 8$	$2(x - 8)$ $2(x + 4)$ $2(x - 4)$ $1(2x - 8)$
6	$10x + 8$	$10(x + 8)$ $2(5x + 4)$ $2(5x - 4)$ $2x(5 + 4)$
8	$9 - 3x$	$3(3 - 3x)$ $1(9 - 3x)$ $3(3 - x)$ $3(3 + x)$
10	$ab + ac$	$a(b - c)$ $a(b + c)$ $a(ab + c)$ $a(b + ac)$

ISBN: 9780170447416

G Factorise the following.

1 $3x + 3y =$ ________________

2 $5x - 5y =$ ________________

3 $2x + 8 =$ ________________

4 $5x - 10 =$ ________________

5 $4x + 12 =$ ________________

6 $4x - 24 =$ ________________

7 $6 + 3x =$ ________________

8 $15 - 5x =$ ________________

9 $xy + yz =$ ________________

10 $2 - 6x =$ ________________

11 $3x + xy =$ ________________

12 $2xy + 4yz =$ ________________

13 $4a + ab =$ ________________

14 $5 + 15y =$ ________________

15 $5xy + 6y =$ ________________

16 $xy + x =$ ________________

17 $h + gh =$ ________________

18 $2ab + 2a =$ ________________

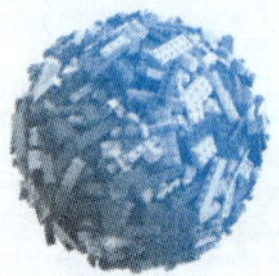

Challenge 3

Factorise the following.

1 $6x + 9 =$ ________________

2 $5x + 5y + 5z =$ ________________

3 $x^2 + 4x =$ ________________

4 $-2x - 10 =$ ________________

5 $-3x + 9 =$ ________________

6 $xy - xz + x^2 =$ ________________

7 $2x^2 + 4x =$ ________________

8 $5xyz - 10xz =$ ________________

9 $x - x^2 =$ ________________

10 $2xy - 4y^2 + x^2y =$ ________________

11 $x^3 + x^2 =$ ________________

12 $2x^2 - 4x + 8x^3 =$ ________________

ISBN: 9780170447416

Find the errors

Some of the following factorisations and expansions are correct and some are incorrect. If the factorisation or expansion is correct, put a tick in the ✓/✗ column. If it is incorrect, put a cross in the ✓/✗ column, and write the correct solution.

		✓/✗	Correct solution
1	$5(d + 4) = 5d + 9$		
2	$10 (2b - 1) = 20b - 10$		
3	$6x + 6 = 6(x - 6)$		
4	$16a + 20 = 4(4a + 5)$		
5	$5(2 + x) = 7 + 5x$		
6	$10d + 10f = 5(2d + 2f)$		
7	$5(x + 5) = 5z + 25$		
8	$4a - 4 = 4(a - 4)$		
9	$12 - 24x = 6(2 - 4x)$		
10	$g(h - f) = gh - f$		
11	$5x - ax = x(5 + a)$		
12	$x^2 + 3x = x(1 + 3)$		
13	$ab + ac - ad = a(b + c + d)$		

ISBN: 9780170447416

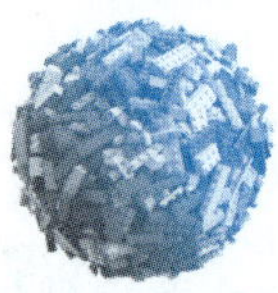

Challenge 4

A Expand and simplify the following.

1 $2(4x + y) =$

2 $-5(x + 4) =$

3 $-3(a - 5) =$

4 $2x(3 + y) =$

5 $-(3x - 6) =$

6 $5x(x - 7) =$

7 $3(2x + 3) + 3(x + 4) =$

8 $2(x - 5) + 3(x - 6) =$

B Factorise the following.

1 $2xyz + 5xy =$

2 $c^3 + 8c =$

3 $a^4 + a - a^2 =$

4 $25pq - 15pqr =$

5 $x + xy - zx =$

6 $8k^2 - 4k + 6k^3 =$

7 $m^5n^2 + m^3n^6 =$

8 $12g^2 + 6g^3 =$

9 $24f - 12f^2 - 30 =$

10 $15r + 30s - 10t =$

ISBN: 9780170447416

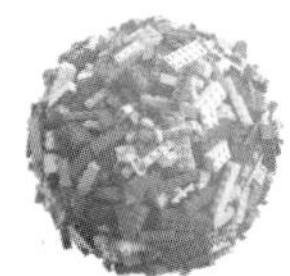

Formulae and substitution

With one variable

What is a formula? A formula is an **algebraic expression** of a **rule**.

Examples:

This is a square with sides L cm long:

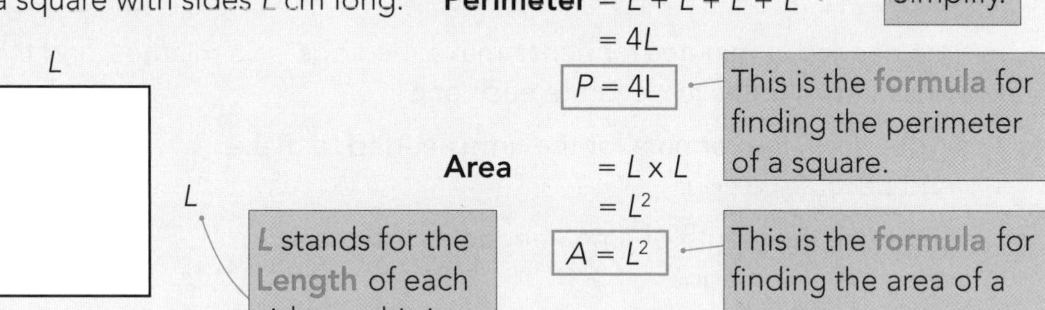

L stands for the **Length** of each side, so this is the **variable**.

Perimeter $= L + L + L + L$ ← Simplify.

$= 4L$

$\boxed{P = 4L}$ ← This is the **formula** for finding the perimeter of a square.

Area $= L \times L$

$= L^2$

$\boxed{A = L^2}$ ← This is the **formula** for finding the area of a square.

What is substitution? Substitution is when you **replace variables with numbers**.

But don't forget **BEDMAS** when doing this.

Examples:

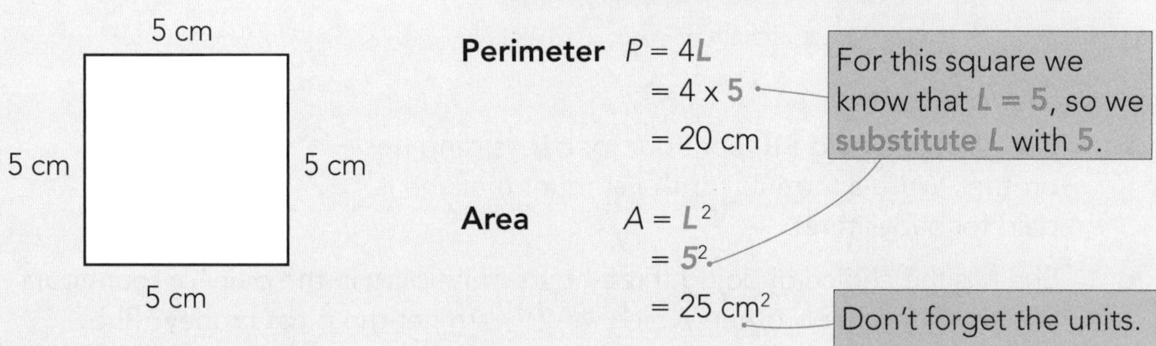

Perimeter $P = 4L$

$= 4 \times 5$ ← For this square we know that $L = 5$, so we **substitute** L with **5**.

$= 20$ cm

Area $A = L^2$

$= 5^2$

$= 25\text{ cm}^2$ ← Don't forget the units.

Some more examples:

1 Angie is making Easter eggs, and the recipe states that she will need 120 g of chocolate for each egg.The formula for the total amount of chocolate she needs is $\boldsymbol{T = 120e}$, where $\boldsymbol{e}$ stands for the **number of eggs**. Calculate the amount of chocolate she needs for seven eggs.

$T = 120e$

$= 120 \times 7$

$= 840$ g

Notice that there should be just **one** '=' sign per line, and they are **lined up** under each other.

2 Battered Buses will charge the school \$150 plus \$2 per passenger to take sports teams to a tournament. The formula for the total fare is $\boldsymbol{C = 150 + 2p}$, where $\boldsymbol{p}$ stands for the **number of passengers**. Calculate the charge for 40 passengers.

$C = 150 + 2p$

$= 150 + 2 \times 40$ ← Replace p by the number of passengers.

$= \$230$

ISBN: 9780170447416

Answer the following.

1 Angie wants to tie a ribbon around each egg. She has calculated that each egg will need 22 cm of ribbon.

a Write down the formula for the total length of ribbon needed for e eggs. $L =$ ____________

b Calculate the length of ribbon needed for her seven eggs. $L =$ ____________

$=$ ____________

$=$ ____________

2 The time needed in minutes for her to make the eggs is 35 minutes, and then it takes her three minutes to decorate each one.

a Write down the formula for the time needed to make and decorate e eggs. $T =$ ____________

b Calculate the length of time needed to make and decorate seven eggs. $T =$ ____________

$=$ ____________

$=$ ____________

3 Cassie earns $12 per hour helping in her parents' dairy. The formula for the amount she gets paid is $A = 12h$, where h stands for the number of hours she has worked.

a How much would she get paid for working four hours? $A =$ ____________

$=$ ____________

$=$ ____________

b She also gets paid $10 per hour for babysitting her brother. Write a formula for the amount that she is paid for babysitting. $A =$ ____________

c She has the choice of doing three hours of helping in the dairy or four hours of babysitting her brother. Which would earn her the most money? Show your calculations.

____

____

____

d When she babysits her cousins, she needs to bike there and back. The formula for the amount her aunt pays her is $A = 13h + 6$ where h stands for the number of hours. Explain how her aunt calculates the amount to pay Cassie.

____

____

e When Mack babysits his cousins, his uncle pays him $12.50 per hour, but he also pays the $3 each way for his bus fare. Write a formula for the amount that he is paid for babysitting. $A =$ ____________

  ISBN: 9780170447416

4 Crummy Coaches will charge $120 to take the sports teams to their tournament, plus $3 for each passenger. Let p stands for the number of passengers.

a Write down the formula for calculating the total charge. $C =$ ______________

b Calculate the charge for taking 35 passengers. $C =$ ______________

$=$ ______________

$=$ ______________

c Compare the charge with that for Battered Buses ($150 plus $2 per passenger). Which one is cheaper for 35 passengers?

____

d Calculate how much the two companies charge (C) for 45 passengers.

Battered Buses: $C =$ ______________ Crummy Coaches: $C =$ ______________

$=$ ______________ $=$ ______________

$=$ ______________ $=$ ______________

e Which company is cheaper, and by how much?

____

f The amount Cruddy Coaches would charge is given by the formula $C = 60 + 5p$, where p stands for the number of passengers. Explain in words what this formula means.

____

____

g Busted Buses charges $70 plus $1 per teacher ($t$) and $5 per student ($s$). Write down the formula for calculating their total charge.

$C =$ ______________

5 Consecutive numbers come one after another; e.g. 4, 5, 6, 7 are consecutive numbers, but 2, 4, 6, 8 are not. If you are given a number (n), the formula for finding the next (N) consecutive number is $N = n + 1$. Use this formula to find the next consecutive number after 13.

$N =$ ______________

$=$ ______________

$=$ ______________

ISBN: 9780170447416

6 Complete the following table.

Formula	$b = 2$	$b = 4$	$b = 10$	$b = 1$
$A = 2b$	$A =$ ____ $=$ ____ $=$ ____	$A =$ ____ $=$ ____ $=$ ____	$A =$ ____ $=$ ____ $=$ ____	$A =$ ____ $=$ ____ $=$ ____
$A = b + 5$	$A =$ ____ $=$ ____ $=$ ____	$A =$ ____ $=$ ____ $=$ ____	$A =$ ____ $=$ ____ $=$ ____	$A =$ ____ $=$ ____ $=$ ____
$A = \frac{20}{b}$	$A =$ ____ $=$ ____ $=$ ____	$A =$ ____ $=$ ____ $=$ ____	$A =$ ____ $=$ ____ $=$ ____	$A =$ ____ $=$ ____ $=$ ____
$A = 45 - b$	$A =$ ____ $=$ ____ $=$ ____	$A =$ ____ $=$ ____ $=$ ____	$A =$ ____ $=$ ____ $=$ ____	$A =$ ____ $=$ ____ $=$ ____
$A = b^2$	$A =$ ____ $=$ ____ $=$ ____	$A =$ ____ $=$ ____ $=$ ____	$A =$ ____ $=$ ____ $=$ ____	$A =$ ____ $=$ ____ $=$ ____
$A = \frac{b + 4}{2}$	$A =$ ____ $=$ ____ $=$ ____	$A =$ ____ $=$ ____ $=$ ____	$A =$ ____ $=$ ____ $=$ ____	$A =$ ____ $=$ ____ $=$ ____

7 If $c = -2$, find the values of the following.

a $3c =$ ________

$=$ ________

b $7 + c =$ ________

$=$ ________

c $c - 4 =$ ________

$=$ ________

d $-3c =$ ________

$=$ ________

e $c^2 =$ ________

$=$ ________

f $c^2 + 3 =$ ________

$=$ ________

$=$ ________

ISBN: 9780170447416

Puzzle

Below is a correctly assembled jigsaw puzzle. Note that each piece fits with another by having equivalent expressions on each edge.

- Study the puzzle to make sure that you understand how it works.
- Take a photograph of it in case you get stuck reassembling it.
- Cut the pieces up and then mix them up.
- Match edges with equivalent expressions in order to reassemble it.

$2a + a$ $a + a$	$3a$ $\frac{a^4}{a}$ $a \div 2$	a^3 $a(a + 2)$ $a \times a$	$a^2 + 2a$ $2 \div a$
$2a$ $a^2 \times a$ $\frac{a^6}{a^4}$	$\frac{a}{2}$ a^3 $a - 2 = 4$ $2a \times 2a$	a^2 $a = 6$ $a + 2 + a - 1$ $2(a + 2)$	$\frac{2}{a}$ $2a + 1$ Double a number
a^2 $a \times 4$ $a(a + 4)$	$4a^2$ $4a$ $a + 2 = 4$ Quadruple a number	$2a + 4$ $a = 2$ $4a + 2 - 2a$ Half of $8a$	$2a$ $2a + 2$ $\frac{4a^2}{2a}$
$a^2 + 4a$ $\frac{a^5}{a^2}$ $a \times 2$	$4a$ a^3 $a \div 2 = 2$ $2a^2 + 2a^2$	$4a$ $a = 4$ $a^2 \times 2 = 8$ $\frac{16a^3}{4a}$	$2a$ $a = 2$ $2a + 2 = 4$
$2a$ $a^3 \div a^2$	$4a^2$ a $2a^2 \times a$	$4a^2$ $2a^3$ $3a + a$	$a = 1$ $4a$

ISBN: 9780170447416

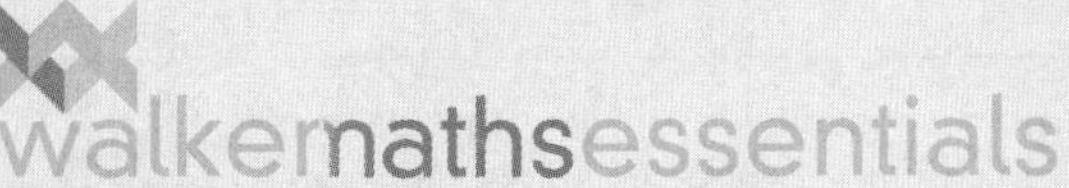
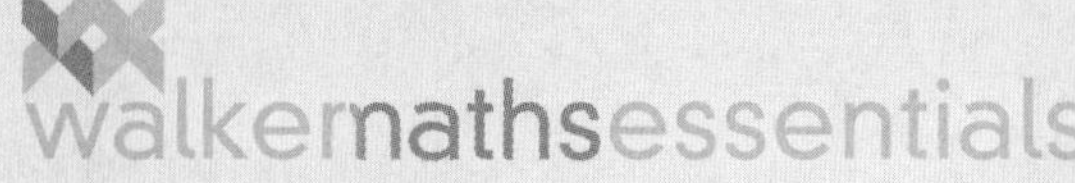

Mix and match

Each of the columns below contain a dark blue instruction header, matching examples of questions (pale blue) and the corresponding answers (white).

- Study the chart to make sure that you understand how it works.
- Take a photograph of it in case you get stuck reassembling it.
- Match five pale blue question boxes to each dark blue instruction header.
- Then match a white answer box to each pale blue question box.

Solve	Evaluate	Expand	Simplify	Factorise
$x + 7 = 12$	If $x = 5$ $2x - 3$	$2(x + y)$	$\frac{4x^3}{2x}$	$2x + 4$
$x = 5$	7	$2x + 2y$	$2x^2$	$2(x + 2)$
$2x - 3 = 17$	If $x = 4$ $x^2 + 12$	$3(x + 2)$	$6x + 3y - 2x - y$	$8 + 4x$
$x = 10$	28	$3x + 6$	$4x + 2y$	$4(2 + x)$
$\frac{x}{6} = 3$	If $x = 2$ and $y = 7$ $3y - x$	$4(2 - x)$	$(3x^4)^2$	$x^2 + 2x$
$x = 18$	19	$8 - 4x$	$9x^8$	$x(x + 2)$
$3x - 4 = 13 + 2x$	If $x = -1$ $3x + 6$	$x(x + y)$	$x \times x$	$xy + zy$
$x = 17$	3	$x^2 + xy$	x^2	$y(x + z)$
$2(x - 2) = 8$	If $x = -2$ and $y = 3$ $\frac{4 - x}{y}$	$3(2x + 3)$	$x + x$	$3x - 6x^2$
$x = 6$	2	$6x + 9$	$2x$	$3x(1 - 2x)$

ISBN: 9780170447416

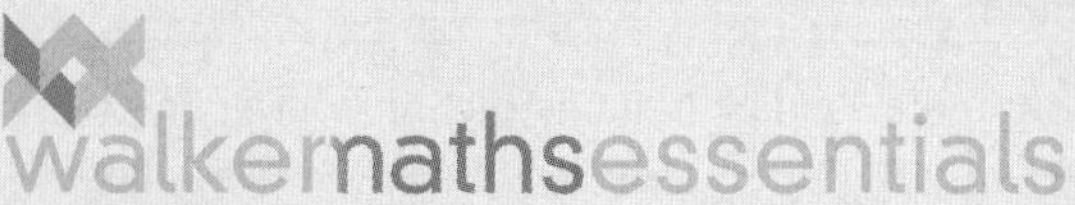

Challenge 5

Complete the following table.

Formula	$b = 2, c = 2$	$b = 4, c = 1$	$b = 5, c = -1$
$A = b + c$	$A =$ ____ $=$ ____ $=$ ____	$A =$ ____ $=$ ____ $=$ ____	$A =$ ____ $=$ ____ $=$ ____
$A = 4c - b$	$A =$ ____ $=$ ____ $=$ ____	$A =$ ____ $=$ ____ $=$ ____	$A =$ ____ $=$ ____ $=$ ____
$A = b(c + 2)$	$A =$ ____ $=$ ____ $=$ ____	$A =$ ____ $=$ ____ $=$ ____	$A =$ ____ $=$ ____ $=$ ____
$A = b^2 + c$	$A =$ ____ $=$ ____ $=$ ____	$A =$ ____ $=$ ____ $=$ ____	$A =$ ____ $=$ ____ $=$ ____
$A = 2b^2$	$A =$ ____ $=$ ____ $=$ ____	$A =$ ____ $=$ ____ $=$ ____	$A =$ ____ $=$ ____ $=$ ____
$A = \frac{b + c}{2}$	$A =$ ____ $=$ ____ $=$ ____	$A =$ ____ $=$ ____ $=$ ____	$A =$ ____ $=$ ____ $=$ ____
$A = \frac{c + b}{c}$	$A =$ ____ $=$ ____ $=$ ____	$A =$ ____ $=$ ____ $=$ ____	$A =$ ____ $=$ ____ $=$ ____

ISBN: 9780170447416

Challenge 6

Substitute with the following values in order to complete the cross-number:

$w = 14$ $y = 2$ $z = 5$

Do the working needed for these in your exercise book.

	1	2		3		
4						5
6			7		8	
		9				
10					11	12
		13		14		
	15			16		

Across		Down	
1	$w - y$	**2**	wy
3	z^2	**3**	$4z + y$
6	$yz + w$	**4**	$3w$
8	$3(w - z)$	**5**	$y + 3z$
9	wyz	**7**	$(yz)^2 + 3w$
10	$\frac{10 + w}{2}$	**10**	$3 + zy$
11	$2w - z$	**12**	$w \div y \times z$
15	$(z + y)^2$	**13**	$3z + 2y$
16	$(z - y)w$	**14**	$y^2 + yz$

ISBN: 9780170447416

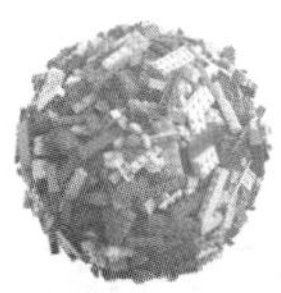

Understanding instructions in algebra

How do I recognise when to ...?	Example	What do I do?	What should the answer look like?
Solve	5 + ♥ = 9 When you have an unknown symbol or letter.	Finding the value of a symbol or letter. 5 + ♥ = 9 ♥ = 4	Variable = constant. ♥ = 4
Evaluate (substitute)	$x + 3$ when $x = 7$ You are told the value of a variable.	Substitute the value for the variable. $x + 3 = 7 + 3$ $= 10$	A constant. 10
Expand	$2(b + 5)$ Contains brackets.	Multiply every term that is inside the brackets by the term outside. $2(b + 5)$ $= 2b + 10$	An expression with no brackets. $2b + 10$
Simplify	Adding/subtracting $a - b + a + 2b$ Contains a mixture of like and unlike terms.	Combine like terms. $a - b + a + 2b$ $= 2a + b$	An expression containing no like terms. $2a + b$
	Multiplying/dividing $\frac{a^2b^3}{ab}$ The same variable occurs in more than one place.	Add or subtract indices for each variable that occurs more than once. $\frac{a^2b^3}{ab} = \frac{a \times a \times b \times b \times b}{a \times b} = ab^2$	An expression in which each variable occurs no more than once. ab^2
Factorise	$5a - 15$ Several terms containing common factors. The terms are added and/or subtracted.	Put the common factor outside the bracket. Divide each term by the common factor to find what goes inside the brackets. $5a - 15 = 5(a - 3)$	An expression with brackets. **No common factors inside the brackets.** $5(a - 3)$

ISBN: 9780170447416

Write the most appropriate instruction (**Solve**, **Evaluate**, **Expand**, **Simplify** or **Factorise**) for each question. Then follow your chosen instruction in order to answer the question.

	Question	Instruction	Answer
1	$16 - ⌘ = 3$	Solve	
2	$p + f + 2p + f$		
3	$2(a - 4)$		
4	$\frac{y^6}{y^4}$		
5	$3x + 6$		
6	$4x + 2$, where $x = 3$		
7	$(3x^2)^2$		
8	$b \times 9 = 45$		

 ISBN: 9780170447416

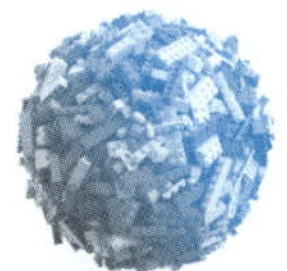

Solving linear equations

- 'Solve' means '**find the value for x**'.

Rules:
1. You can do anything you like to an equation as long as you do the **same to both sides**.
2. There should be only **one equals sign** per line.
3. Collect all the variables on one side and numbers on the other side.
4. When you want to get rid of something, perform the **opposite** operation.
5. Your aim is to get **x = ...**

One-step equations – adding and subtracting

Examples:

1

$$y + 7 = 11$$

We need to get rid of the **+ 7** from the left side.

$$y + 7 - 7 = 11 - 7$$

Do the **opposite** of **+ 7**. **Subtract 7** from **both** sides.

$$y = 4$$

This is our aim: to have the variable on the left and its value on the right.

Notice that there should be just **one** '=' sign per line, and they are **lined up** under each other.

We can always **check** that the solution works: **4** + 7 = 11 ✓

2

$$m - 3 = 9$$

We need to get rid of the **– 3** from the left side.

$$m - 3 + 3 = 9 + 3$$

Do the **opposite** of **– 3**. **Add 3** to **both** sides.

$$m = 12$$

We can always **check** that the solution works: **12** – 3 = 9 ✓

Solve the following, showing all the steps in the working.

1 $a - 6 = 4$

__________ = __________

a = __________

2 $b + 9 = 12$

__________ = __________

b = __________

3 $n + 3 = 9$

________ = ________

$n =$ ________

4 $u + 2 = 8$

________ = ________

$u =$ ________

5 $y - 6 = 10$

________ = ________

$y =$ ________

6 $a + 4 = 7$

________ = ________

$a =$ ________

7 $x + 10 = 25$

________ = ________

$x =$ ________

8 $x - 10 = 32$

________ = ________

$x =$ ________

9 $x - 3 = 7$

10 $x + 4 = 24$

11 $y + 3 = 27$

12 $p - 9 = 15$

13 $v + 5 = 5$

14 $x + 6 = 2$

15 $5 - x = 3$

16 $1 - y = -2$

 ISBN: 9780170447416

An extra trick:
Sometimes the **variable** is on the **right**-hand side. Example: $5 = y + 3$.
Because both sides are equal to each other, you can **flip** them around:

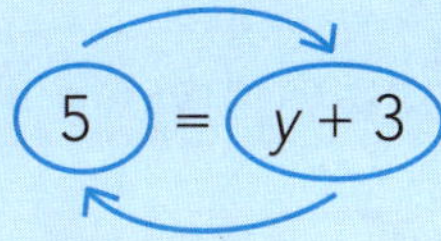

so $y + 3 = 5$

17 $8 = h - 10$

18 $3 = x + 2$

19 $16 = p + 9$

20 $5 = t - 7$

21 $12 = z - 3$

22 $12 = x + 3$

23 $4 = y - 6$

24 $95 = q + 10$

25 $11 = 2 - x$

26 $20 = 7 - y$

ISBN: 9780170447416

One-step equations – multiplying and dividing

Examples:

1 $\frac{p}{2} = 5$

We need to get rid of the ÷ 2 from the left side.

$\frac{p}{2} \times \frac{2}{1} = 5 \times \frac{2}{1}$

Do the **opposite** of ÷ 2. **Multiply both** sides by 2 (or $\frac{2}{1}$ if you are dealing with fractions).

$p = 10$

2 $5f = 20$

Remember, $5f$ means $5 \times f$. We need to get rid of the × 5 from the left side.

$\frac{5f}{5} = \frac{20}{5}$

Do the **opposite** of × 5. **Divide both** sides by 5.

$f = 4$

Solve the following, showing all the steps in the working.

1 $\frac{u}{3} = 5$

__________ = __________

u = __________

2 $2 \times f = 20$

__________ = __________

f = __________

3 $3n = 12$

__________ = __________

n = __________

4 $\frac{a}{4} = 5$

__________ = __________

a = __________

5 $2x = 100$

__________ = __________

x = __________

6 $\frac{b}{5} = 6$

__________ = __________

b = __________

ISBN: 9780170447416

7 $\frac{x}{2} = 7$

________ = ________

$x =$ ________

8 $4x = 24$

________ = ________

$x =$ ________

9 $2x = 16$

10 $\frac{x}{4} = 3$

11 $3y = 21$

12 $9p = 27$

13 $\frac{x}{10} = 3$

14 $x \div 4 = 7$

15 $2y = 6$

16 $\frac{x}{6} = -3$

17 $\frac{m}{5} = 2$

18 $3y = -12$

ISBN: 9780170447416

Remember the trick:
Sometimes the **variable** is on the **right**-hand side. Example: $30 = 2w$.
Because both sides are equal to each other, you can **flip** them around:

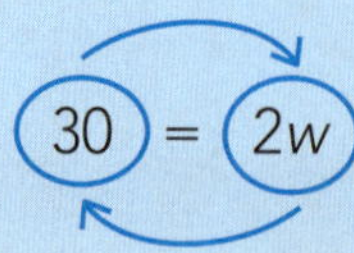

so $2w = 30$

19 $2 = \frac{x}{4}$

20 $6 = 2g$

21 $24 = 6x$

22 $10 = \frac{p}{3}$

23 $16 = 8z$

24 $120 = 12f$

25 $4 = 4a$

26 $-12 = 3q$

27 $-12 = 6d$

28 $5 = \frac{-y}{3}$

 ISBN: 9780170447416

Mixing it up

1 $x + 4 = 18$

2 $2a = 12$

3 $x - 5 = 14$

4 $\frac{a}{6} = 2$

5 $4b = 20$

6 $x - 6 = 9$

7 $x + 8 = 24$

8 $\frac{y}{5} = 3$

9 $3a = 21$

10 $x - 3 = 23$

11 $x + 12 = 27$

12 $\frac{b}{6} = 6$

ISBN: 9780170447416

Find the errors

Some of the following equations are solved correctly and some aren't. If the equation is solved correctly, put a tick in the ✓/✗ column. If not, put a cross in the ✓/✗ column, highlight the mistake, and write the correct solution.

		✓/✗	Correct solution
1	$x - 6 = 10$ $x = 10 - 6$ $x = 4$		
2	$6x = 18$ $x = \frac{16}{8}$ $x = 2$		
3	$\frac{x}{2} = 50$ $x = 50 \times 2$ $x = 100$		
4	$x + 3 = 8$ $x = 8 - 3$ $x = 6$		
5	$3x = 21$ $x = \frac{21}{3}$ $x = 7$		
6	$\frac{x}{2} = 17$ $x = 17 + 2$ $x = 19$		

 ISBN: 9780170447416

Mixing it up

Do the working needed to complete the cross-number in your exercise book.

	1	2		3		
4						5
6			7		8	
		9				
10					11	12
		13		14		
	15			16		

Across		Down	
1	$x - 3 = 18$	**2**	$x \div 6 = 3$
3	$2x = 20$	**3**	$x + 1 = 17$
6	$\frac{x}{6} = 4$	**4**	$x - 4 = 28$
8	$7 + x = 18$	**5**	$7 = x \div 3$
9	$400 = 4x$	**7**	$102 = x - 99$
10	$29 = x + 7$	**10**	$\frac{x}{5} = 5$
11	$4x = 48$	**12**	$x - 19 = 4$
15	$x + 1 = 72$	**13**	$41 = x - 0$
16	$39 = 3x$	**14**	$3 = \frac{x}{17}$

ISBN: 9780170447416

Forming then solving linear equations

Write an equation for each of the following, and then solve it to find the mystery number. Use the variable x to represent the number.

1 Multiply a number by four to get twenty.

$4x = 20$

$\frac{4x}{4} = \frac{20}{4}$

$x = 5$

2 Divide a number by three to get five.

3 A number plus five is eight.

4 A number reduced by two is twelve.

5 A number shared equally between three is ten.

6 A number multiplied by six is twelve.

7 Double a number is fourteen.

8 Dividing a number by two is eight.

9 Three less than a number is nine.

10 Four more than a number is six.

 ISBN: 9780170447416

Challenge 7

Solve the following equations.

1 $2x = 5$

2 $x + 8 = 2$

3 $2 + x = 9$

4 $\frac{x}{3} = -6$

5 $1(x + 5) = 12$

6 A tenth of a number equals thirty.

7 $\frac{x}{-4} = -6$

8 $9x = 3$

ISBN: 9780170447416

Two-step equations

- First collect all the terms with variables (e.g. x) on the left, and all the numbers on the right.
- Do the adding or subtracting **before** the multiplying or dividing.

Examples:

1

$$2x - 3 = 11$$

$$2x - 3 + 3 = 11 + 3$$

First adding/subtracting: add 3 to both sides.

$$2x = 14$$

$$\frac{2x}{2} = \frac{14}{2}$$

Then multiplying/dividing: divide both sides by 2.

$$x = 7$$

2

$$4x + 2 = 14$$

$$4x + 2 - 2 = 14 - 2$$

First adding/subtracting: subtract 2 from both sides.

$$4x = 12$$

$$\frac{4x}{4} = \frac{12}{4}$$

Then multiplying/dividing: divide both sides by 4.

$$x = 3$$

Solve the following.

1 $2x - 3 = 7$

2 $3a + 4 = 13$

3 $4y + 3 = 15$

4 $5z - 5 = 25$

5 $6p - 3 = 9$

6 $10d + 2 = 22$

ISBN: 9780170447416

7 $2b - 7 = 5$

8 $7x + 4 = 25$

9 $4t - 4 = 12$

10 $3g - 2 = 22$

11 $5a - 2 = 18$

12 $3x - 1 = 5$

13 $4p + 1 = 9$

14 $5y - 3 = 17$

15 $20x - 20 = 80$

16 $6g - 15 = 15$

17 $5a - 25 = 0$

18 $3x - 3 = 6$

ISBN: 9780170447416

Find the errors

Some of the following equations are solved correctly and some aren't. If the equation is solved correctly, put a tick in the ✓/✗ column. If not, put a cross in the ✓/✗ column, highlight the mistake, and write the correct solution.

		✓/✗	Correct solution
1	$2g + 2 = 14$ $2g = 14 + 2$ $g = \frac{16}{2}$ $g = 8$		
2	$3p - 3 = 27 + p$ $2p = 27 + 3$ $p = \frac{30}{2}$ $p = 15$		
3	$4x + 6 = 30$ $4x = 30 - 6$ $x = \frac{24}{4}$ $x = 6$		
4	$6x - 2 = 10$ $6x = 12$ $x = \frac{6}{12}$ $x = \frac{1}{2}$		
5	$9x + 2 = 38$ $9x = 38 - 2$ $x = \frac{36}{9}$ $x = 4$		
6	$5y - 3 = 2$ $5y = 2 + 3$ $y = 5 \times 5$ $y = 25$		

 ISBN: 9780170447416

Forming then solving two-step linear equations

Write an equation for each of the following, and then solve it to find the mystery number. Use the variable x to represent the number.

1 If a number is doubled, and then three is subtracted, the answer is seven.

2 A number is multiplied by three, and then one is added. The answer is ten.

3 Multiply a number by four, and then two is added to it. The answer is eighteen.

4 Multiply a number by three, and then it is decreased by three. The answer is six.

5 Four is added to a number after it is doubled. The answer is ten.

6 A number is multiplied by three, and then two is subtracted. The answer is one.

Write equations for the following situations, using the variables in brackets. Then solve the equation in order to answer the question.

7 Bernie had $50 and began to save $12 a week until he had $182. For how many weeks (w) did he save?

8 Grace bought avocados for $2.25 each and received $1.50 change from $15. How many avocados ($a$) did she buy?

9 One group of students is three times as large as another (x). Altogether there are sixteen students. How big are the two groups?

10 When Alfred doubles his lucky number and adds five, he gets an answer of thirty-one. What is his lucky number (x)?

ISBN: 9780170447416

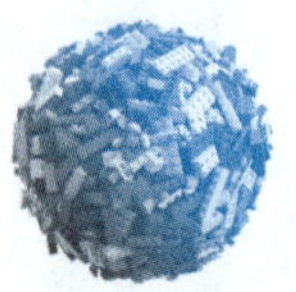

Challenge 8

Find the unknown number for each of the following.

1 $5 = 2y - 5$

2 $\frac{x}{3} - 4 = 2$

3 $2x + 8 = 4$

4 $4 + \frac{x}{3} = 6$

5 $2(x + 3) = 15$

6 $\frac{x + 4}{2} = 6$

7 $-2x + 3 = 1$

8 A number is decreased by two, then divided by five. The answer is three.

 ISBN: 9780170447416

With variables on both sides

- Remember, **first** add and/or subtract to collect all the terms with variables (e.g. x) on the left, and all the numbers on the right.
- **Then** do any multiplying or dividing needed.

Examples:

1

$$5x = 12 + \mathbf{x}$$
$$5x - \mathbf{x} = 12 + x - \mathbf{x}$$
$$\mathbf{4}x = 12$$
$$\frac{4x}{\mathbf{4}} = \frac{12}{\mathbf{4}}$$
$$x = 3$$

First adding/subtracting: **subtract x** from both sides.

Then multiplying/dividing: **divide** both sides by **4**.

2

$$5 + 2x = \mathbf{4x} + 1$$
$$5 + 2x - \mathbf{4x} = 4x + 1 - \mathbf{4x}$$
$$5 - 2x = 1$$
$$5 - 2x - \mathbf{5} = 1 - \mathbf{5}$$
$$-2x = -4$$
$$\frac{-2x}{\mathbf{2}} = \frac{-4}{\mathbf{-2}}$$
$$x = 2$$

First adding/subtracting: **subtract 4x** from both sides. Then **subtract 5** from both sides.

Notice that now we have just an x term on the left and a constant on the right.

Then multiplying/dividing: **divide** both sides by **–2**.

Solve the following.

1 $3x = 6 + 2x$

2 $5y = 2 + 4y$

3 $4x = 12 + 2x$

4 $5a = 8 + 3a$

ISBN: 9780170447416

5 $b = 8 - b$

6 $6y = 10 + 4y$

7 $3a = 15 - 2a$

8 $2a + 1 = 7 + a$

9 $8g - 2 = 7g + 1$

10 $4c - 8 = 3c + 2$

11 $3p - 2 = 8 + p$

12 $6y - 1 = 8 + 3y$

13 $6x - 1 = 4x + 3$

14 $f + 2 + 2f = 18 - f$

15 $1 + 2x = 26 - 3x$

16 $-3 + x = 9 + 4x$

ISBN: 9780170447416

Find the errors

Some of the following equations are solved correctly and some aren't. If the equation is solved correctly, put a tick in the ✓/✗ column. If not, put a cross in the ✓/✗ column, highlight the mistake, and write the correct solution.

		✓/✗	Correct solution
1	$5a = 12 + a$ $6a = 12$ $a = \frac{12}{6}$ $a = 2$		
2	$3p - 6 = p$ $3p = 6$ $p = \frac{6}{3}$ $p = 2$		
3	$4a - 5 = a + 4$ $3a - 5 = 4$ $3a = 9$ $a = 3$		
4	$x - 1 = 8 - x$ $2x - 1 = 8$ $2x = 8$ $x = 4$		
5	$5b - 4 = 10 - 2b$ $7b - 4 = 10$ $7b = 14$ $b = 2$		
6	$2 + 4z = 2z + 6$ $4z = 2z + 4$ $2z = 4$ $z = \frac{2}{4}$		

ISBN: 9780170447416

With brackets

- Expand the brackets first, before solving the same way as you did in the last exercise.

The order of operations for solving an equation:

1. **Expand the brackets**
2. **Add/subtract like terms**
3. **Multiply/divide.**

Examples:

1

$$5(x-1) = 15$$
$$5x - 5 = 15$$
$$5x - 5 + 5 = 15 + 5$$
$$5x = 20$$
$$\frac{5x}{5} = \frac{20}{5}$$
$$x = 4$$

1 **Expand** the brackets.

2 Add/subtract
Add 5 to both sides.

3 Multiply/divide
Divide both sides by **5**.

2

$$-2(3x-4) = 26$$
$$-6x + 8 = 26$$
$$-6x + 8 - 8 = 26 - 8$$
$$-6x = 18$$
$$\frac{-6x}{-6} = \frac{18}{-6}$$
$$x = -3$$

1 **Expand** the brackets.

2 Add/subtract
Subtract 8 from both sides.

3 Multiply/divide
Divide both sides by **−6**.

Solve the following.

1 $2(x + 4) = 20$

2 $3(x - 2) = 12$

 ISBN: 9780170447416

3 $6(x + 2) = 18$

4 $3(x - 4) = 18$

5 $3(x + 3) = 18$

6 $4(x - 1) = 16$

7 $2(5 + x) = 24$

8 $3(4 + x) = 36$

9 $2(2x + 3) = 10$

10 $3(2x - 5) = 15$

11 $4(2x - 3) = 20$

12 $-2(7 - x) = 10$

ISBN: 9780170447416

Find the errors

Some of the following equations are solved correctly and some aren't. If the equation is solved correctly, put a tick in the ✓/✗ column. If not, put a cross in the ✓/✗ column, highlight the mistake, and write the correct solution.

		✓/✗	Correct solution
1	$2(x-4)=10$ $2x-8=10$ $2x=18$ $x=9$		
2	$5(x+5)=25$ $5x+15=25$ $5x=40$ $x=8$		
3	$4(3+x)=36$ $12+4x=36$ $4x=24$ $x=6$		
4	$2(x+3)=12$ $2x+6=12$ $2x=6$ $x=\frac{2}{6}$		
5	$2(3x-8)=20$ $6x-16=20$ $6x=36$ $x=6$		
6	$2(5+2x)=18$ $10+4x=18$ $4x=8$ $x=2$		

 ISBN: 9780170447416

Mixing it up

Do the working needed to complete the cross-number in your exercise book.

	1	2		3		
4						5
6			7		8	
		9				
10					11	12
		13		14		
	15			16		

Across		**Down**	
1	$x - 4 = 8$	**2**	$\frac{x}{3} = 7$
3	$2x + 3 = 25$	**3**	$2x + 4 = x + 19$
6	$x + 5 = 22$	**4**	$2x - 10 = 32$
8	$4x = 40$	**5**	$3(x + 5) = 75$
9	$\frac{x}{4} = 26$	**7**	$4 + x = 210$
10	$3x = x + 30$	**10**	$4x - 5 = 35$
11	$2(2 + x) = 28$	**12**	$44 = 2x$
15	$18 = x - 5$	**13**	$4 + 2x = x + 17$
16	$13 = \frac{x}{2}$	**14**	$2(x - 11) = 22$

ISBN: 9780170447416

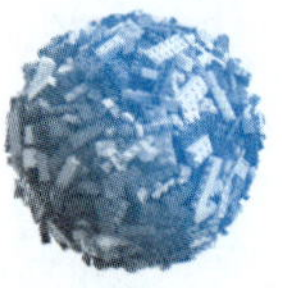

Challenge 9

Solve the following.

1 $\frac{x-2}{3} = 4$

2 $\frac{x}{3} + 4 = 19$

3 $2(b-7) = b + 1$

4 $2(a+4) + 2 = 16$

5 $-3p = p - 10$

6 $-2(y-3) = 18$

7 The perimeter of this triangle is 20 cm. Calculate the length of the unknown sides.

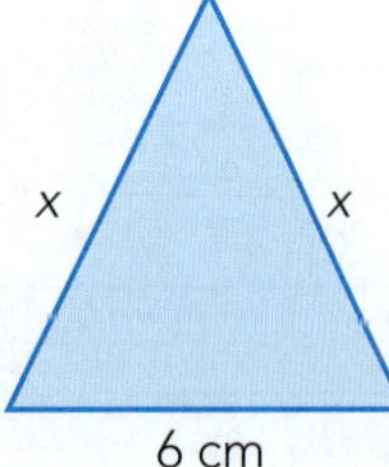

8 The perimeter of this rectangle is 36 m. Calculate the length of the unknown sides.

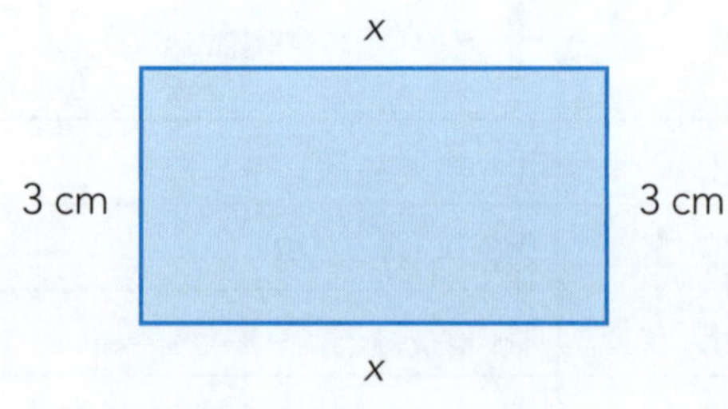

 ISBN: 9780170447416

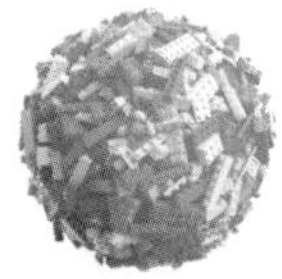

Understanding instructions in algebra

How do I recognise when to ...?	Example	What do I do?	What should the answer look like?
Solve	$2x + 3 = 7$ Contains an '=' sign.	Shift terms with variables to the left, and constants to the right. $2x + 3 = 7$ (–3) $2x = 4$ (÷2) $x = 2$	Variable = constant. $x = 2$
Evaluate	$2x + 3$ when $x = 7$ You are told the value of a variable.	Substitute the value for the variable. $2x + 3 = 2(7) + 3$ $= 14 + 3$ $= 17$	A constant. 17
Expand	$2a(5a + b - 1)$ Contains brackets.	Multiply every term that is inside the brackets by the term outside. $2a(5a + b - 1)$ $= 10a^2 + 2ab - 2a$	An expression with no brackets. $10a^2 + 2ab - 2a$
Simplify	Adding/subtracting $3a + b + a^2 - 2a - 6b$ Contains a mixture of like and unlike terms.	Combine like terms. $3a + b + a^2 - 2a - 6b$ $= a + a^2 - 5b$	An expression containing no like terms. $a + a^2 - 5b$
	Multiplying/dividing $\frac{12ab^5}{3a^3bc}$ The same variable occurs in more than one place.	Add or subtract indices for each variable that occurs more than once. $\frac{12ab^5}{3a^3bc} = \frac{4b^4}{a^2c}$	An expression in which each variable occurs no more than once. $\frac{4b^4}{a^2c}$
Factorise	$20a^2b - 5ab$ Several terms containing common factors. The terms are added and/or subtracted.	Put the common factor outside the bracket. Divide each term by the common factor to find what goes inside the brackets. $20a^2b - 5ab = 5ab(4a - 1)$	An expression with brackets. **No common factors inside the brackets.** $5ab(4a - 1)$

ISBN: 9780170447416

Write the most appropriate instruction (**Solve**, **Evaluate**, **Expand**, **Simplify** or **Factorise**) for each question. Then follow your chosen instruction in order to answer the question.

	Question	Instruction	Answer
1	$5x - 4 = 11$		
2	$3p + 2q + 4p + q$		
3	$2x + 12$		
4	$\frac{8y^2}{2y}$		
5	$3(x - 2)$		
6	$\frac{12}{x}$, where $x = 4$		
7	$(a^4)^2$		
8	$2 \times 3p \times p$		

 ISBN: 9780170447416

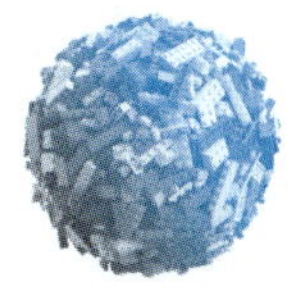

Revision 1

1 Write an expression for this phrase. Use the variable y.

Four less than a number: ____________

2 Write a phrase for this expression:

$3 + p$ ____________________

3 Cody has $56 in his bank account, and he is saving $12 each week from the amount he is paid for caring for his sister after school. The formula for the total amount he has in the bank is given by the expression **Total = 56 + 12w**.

a The variable is ____ and it stands for ______________________________.

b Use the expression to calculate how much he has in his account after four weeks.

____

4 Simplify the following expressions.

a $p \times p \times 2 =$ ____________

b $\frac{10}{2y} =$ ____________

c $3g + 2h + g - h =$ ____________

d $e + 3e + f + 2f - 2e =$ ____________

e $2y \times 3y =$ ____________

f $\frac{a^5b^3}{a^3b} =$ ____________

g $(5g^3)^2 =$ ____________

h $\frac{15z^2}{3z} - z =$ ____________

5 Expand the following expressions.

a $3(y + 2) =$ ____________

b $2(6 - x) =$ ____________

6 Factorise the following expressions.

a $7p + 14 =$ ____________

b $2t^2 + 6t =$ ____________

7 Complete the table.

Formula	$d = 3$	$d = 6$	$d = 1$	$d = 0$
$A = 32 - d$	$A =$ ______	$A =$ ______	$A =$ ______	$A =$ ______

8 Jenny visits the local mountain bike park. She pays $20 for a day pass and if she chooses to use the chairlift it costs $3.50 a time.

The formula for how much it will cost her takes the form $C = 20 + 3.5r$, where:

- C stands for the total cost in dollars,
- r stands for the number of times she uses the chairlift.

a Jenny thinks that she would like to use the chairlift three times. How much would it cost her?

$C = 20 + 3.5r =$ ______________

$=$ ______________

Jenny's friend Mona goes for the unlimited chairlift pass, which costs her $34 for the day.

b If they use the chairlift only twice, who has spent less money?

Jenny

$C = 20 + 3.5r =$ ______________

$=$ ______________

Mona

$=$ ______________

____

c How many chairlift rides would Mona need to take to get the most out of her money?

____

____

____

____

9 Solve the following equations.

a $p - 4 = 9$

____

____

____

b $30 = 5p$

____

____

____

c $3f - 2 = 13$

____

____

____

d $2y + 3 = 11$

____

____

____

e $4x = 2x + 16$

____

____

____

f $3(x + 2) = 27$

____

____

____

 ISBN: 9780170447416

10 Write and solve equations for each of the following. Use x as your variable.

a Double a number is twelve.

____

____

b Five less than a number is nine.

____

____

c A number is doubled, then two is added. The answer is eight.

____

____

____

d Multiplying a number by three, then decreased by two. The answer is sixteen.

____

____

____

11 Write the most appropriate instruction (Solve, Evaluate, Expand, Simplify or Factorise) for each question. Then follow your chosen instruction in order to answer the question.

	Question	Instruction	Answer
a	$2(p - 4)$	______________	______________________
b	$2(s + 3)$, if $s = 3$	______________	______________________ ______________________
c	$3x - 4 = 23$	______________	______________________ ______________________
d	$2p + 16$	______________	______________________ ______________________

ISBN: 9780170447416

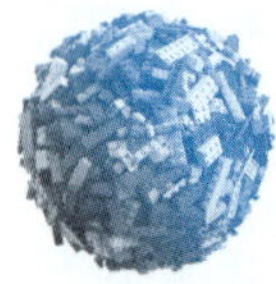

Revision 2

1 Write an expression for this phrase. Use the variable y. Seven more than a number. __________

2 Write a phrase for this expression:

$\frac{2}{y}$ ____________________

3 Cyril takes 20 minutes to get himself ready for school in the morning. His job is to feed the animals in the morning, which takes two minutes per animal. The formula for the total time he needs before leaving home is **Total = 20 + 2*a***.

a The variable is ____ and it stands for ____________________.

b Use the expression to calculate how long he needs to allow if he has three animals to feed.

____

4 Simplify the following expressions.

a $4 \times y \times 2 =$ __________ **b** $\frac{4p}{20} =$ __________

c $5p + 2g - 2p + g =$ __________ **d** $3a + 4b - a - 2b =$ __________

e $4p \times 5m =$ __________ **f** $\frac{c^6d^2}{c^3d} =$ __________

g $(2b^2)^3 =$ __________ **h** $\frac{21y^3}{3y} =$ __________

5 Expand the following expressions.

a $2(x - 3) =$ __________ **b** $p(m + n) =$ __________

6 Factorise the following expressions.

a $3x + 12 =$ __________ **b** $xy + xz =$ __________

7 Complete the table.

Formula	$d = 2$	$d = 4$	$d = 32$	$d = 0$
$A = \frac{d}{2}$	$A =$ ______	$A =$ ______	$A =$ ______	$A =$ ______

 ISBN: 9780170447416

8 Harry is paid to help his elderly neighbours to do jobs around the house. They pay him $13 per hour.

The formula for how much he earns is $T = 13h$, where:

- T stands for the total Harry earns,
- h stands for the number of hours he works.

a How much would Harry get paid for five hours of work?

$T = 13h =$ ______________

$=$ ______________

Harry also gets paid $8 for walking the dog for 30 minutes.

b If Harry is to walk the dog for one hour each day for a week and does eight hours of work for his neighbour, which chore will earn him more money?

Neighbour jobs

$T = 13h =$ ______________

$=$ ______________

Dog walking

$=$ ______________

$=$ ______________

____

9 Solve the following equations.

a $y + 6 = 14$

b $7 = \frac{p}{4}$

c $2b + 3 = 17$

d $3a - 4 = 11$

e $3y = 16 - y$

f $2(x - 2) = 18$

ISBN: 9780170447416

10 Write and solve equations for each of the following. Use x as your variable.

a Half a number is nine.

b Three more than a number is ten.

c Two is added to a number after it is doubled. The answer is six.

d Multiply a number by four, then three is subtracted. The answer is nine.

11 Write the most appropriate instruction (Solve, Evaluate, Expand, Simplify or Factorise) for each question. Then follow your chosen instruction in order to answer the question.

	Question	Instruction	Answer
a	$2p + r - p + 3r$		
b	$(2y)^2$		
c	$4(x + 3)$		
d	$2x + 3 = 13$		

 ISBN: 9780170447416

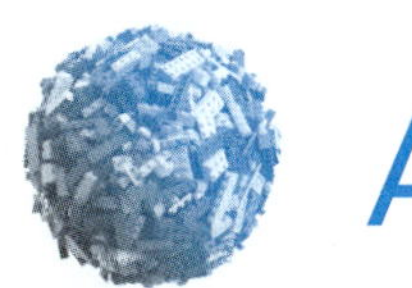

Answers

Revision (pp. 6–8)

Working with integers (pp. 6–7)

Multiplying and dividing intergers

1	30	**2**	−20
3	8	**4**	5
5	−3	**6**	2
7	−24	**8**	−2
9	−12	**10**	12
11	2	**12**	−24

Adding and subtracting integers

1	2	**2**	−7
3	−4	**4**	−2
5	2	**6**	1
7	5	**8**	−6
9	−1	**10**	0
11	0	**12**	−8
13	10	**14**	−1

Order of operations (p. 8)

B Brackets
E Exponents
D Division
M Multiplication
A Addition
S Subtraction

1	15	**2**	38
3	7	**4**	9
5	−5	**6**	12
7	10	**8**	21
9	4	**10**	2
11	2	**12**	−4
13	2	**14**	−10
15	−9	**16**	3
17	13	**18**	−2
19	−5	**20**	6
21	−6	**22**	4

The language of algebra (pp. 9–14)

From words to expressions (p. 9)

+ add, more, plus, sum, total
x multiply, times, lots of, product
– subtract, minus, less than, take away, decrease
÷ divide, goes into, division, split

1	$n + 4$	**2**	$n - 2$
3	$5 - n$	**4**	$2n$
5	$n \div 9$ or $\frac{n}{9}$	**6**	$n - 3$
7	$2n + 1$	**8**	$(n - 3) \div 2$ or $\frac{n-3}{2}$
9	$n - 2$	**10**	$2n - 2$

Finding the value of a symbol (pp. 10–11)

1	♣ = 4	**2**	✶ = 4
3	♥ = 3	**4**	☺ = 7
5	⌘ = 3	**6**	✠ = 1
7	$c = 7$	**8**	$s = 12$
9	$h = 11$	**10**	$w = 3$
11	$L = 4$	**12**	$c = 3$

1	♥ = 8	**2**	⌘ = 4
3	♣ = 2	**4**	☺ = 5
5	✶ = 2	**6**	✠ = 3
7	$h = 5$	**8**	$y = 9$
9	$p = 3$	**10**	$b = 4$
11	$L = 4$	**12**	$c = 8$
13	$g = 5$	**14**	$d = 4$

15

	✓/✗	Correct solution
1	✗	4 + 6 – 1 = 9
2	✗	14 – 2 – 2 = 10 ♥ = 2
3	✓	
4	✗	6 + 6 + 3 = 15 ✠ = 6
5	✓	
6	✗	2 + 1 x 3 = 2 + 3 = 5

Phrases to expressions (pp. 12–14)

1	$2f$	**2**	$e - 3$
3	$f + e$	**4**	$f \div 3$ or $\frac{f}{3}$
5	$e + 2$	**6**	$\frac{f}{2}$
7	$e - f$	**8**	$f \div 3$ or $\frac{f}{3}$
9	$3 - f$	**10**	$e + f$
11	$\frac{2}{f}$	**12**	$f - 2$
13	$2e$	**14**	$f - e$
15	$f \times f$	**16**	$f + e$

1	$y + 10$	**2**	$y \div 3$ or $\frac{y}{3}$
3	$4y$	**4**	$y - 1$
5	$2y$	**6**	$y + 3$
7	$y - 8$	**8**	$12 \div y$ or $\frac{12}{y}$
9	$2y - 3$	**10**	$(y - 1) \div 3$ or $\frac{y-1}{3}$

11 A number with two added to it

12 A number taken off four
13 A number divided by two
14 Six times a number
15 A number subtracted from twelve
16 Three divided by a number
17 A number multiplied by one with four subtracted from it
18 Double a number then another number taken away

Challenge 1 (p. 15)

1

 = 10

 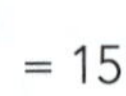 = 15

 = 20

2

 = 30

 = 20

 = 15

3

 = 9

 = 10

 = 15

More about variables (p. 16)

1 **a** The variable is ***h*** and it stands for **the number of hours**.
b $45
2 **a** The variable is ***f*** and it stands for **the number of friends**.
b 9
3 **a** The variable is ***r*** and it stands for **the number of rows**.
b 11

Simplifying expressions (pp. 17–25)

Multiplying (pp. 17–18)

1	$3a$	**2**	p^3
3	$2af$	**4**	$6g$
5	$8ab$	**6**	$12b^2$
7	y^2	**8**	$6efg$
9	$-4g$	**10**	$-6a$
11	a^2	**12**	bfg
13	$8b$	**14**	$6ce$
15	$-2a$	**16**	$4fs$
17	$15f$	**18**	$6g$
19	$-8p$	**20**	$21pq$
21	$20b$	**22**	$5m^2$
23	f^3	**24**	$2g$
25	$18p^2$	**26**	$16f^2$
27	$-8d$	**28**	$40p$

29

$6 \times a \times b$
$1 \times b \times a \times -6$
$-3 \times 2 \times b$
$2 \times a \times 3 \times a$
$a \times -2 \times -3$
$-2a \times -3 \times -1$
$a \times -6 \times b \times b$
$b \times 6 \times -1 \times b$
$b \times b \times b \times 6$
$2 \times b \times 3$

$-6ab$
$6b^3$
$6a^2$
$-6b^2$
$6b^2$
$6ab$
$-6ab^2$
$6b$
$6a$
$-6b$
$-6a$

The term left over is $6b^2$.

Dividing (pp. 19–20)

1	$\frac{b}{2}$	**2**	$\frac{3}{g}$
3	$\frac{1}{5}a$	**4**	$3d$
5	$\frac{f}{2}$	**6**	$\frac{2}{b}$
7	$\frac{y}{2}$	**8**	$2d$
9	$\frac{4}{e}$	**10**	$\frac{2b}{a}$
11	$\frac{3b}{f}$	**12**	$\frac{g}{2}$
13	$\frac{1}{3p}$	**14**	$\frac{3h}{r}$
15	$3m$	**16**	$\frac{1}{3a}$
17	$\frac{b}{7a}$	**18**	$\frac{2}{w}$
19	$\frac{4z}{v}$	**20**	$-2b$
21	$2p$	**22**	$\frac{5b}{2}$ or $2.5b$

 ISBN: 9780170447416

23

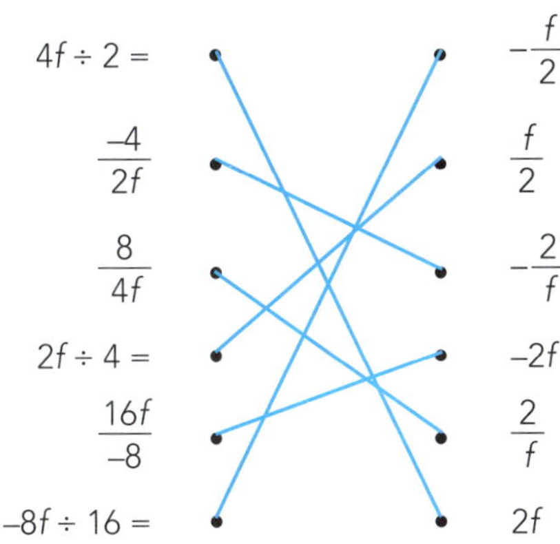

Putting it together (p. 21)

1 p^2
2 $2p$
3 $\frac{p}{2}$
4 $6p$
5 $\frac{1}{6p}$
6 $2mp$
7 $6mp$
8 $\frac{2}{m}$
9 $3p$
10 $-6p$
11 $3mp$
12 $\frac{5}{p}$
13 $5p$
14 $2p^2$
15 $\frac{p}{5}$
16 $2m$

Like terms (p. 22)

1 unlike
2 like
3 like
4 unlike
5 like
6 like
7 like
8 unlike
9 like
10 unlike
11 unlike
12 like
13 unlike
14 like
15 like
16 unlike
17 unlike
18 like
19 like
20 like

Your answers are likely to be different. If you are unsure if they are correct, check with your teacher.

1 $2a, -a, 9a$
2 $g, -g, 5g$
3 $-y^2, 3y^2, 43y^2$
4 $hd, dh, 3hd$
5 $6, 0, -1$
6 $p, 5p, 12p$
7 $x^2, 7x^2, -x^2$
8 $yxz, 4zxy, -xyz$
9 $7m, m, 3m$
10 $we, 4we, 10ew$

Adding and subtracting (pp. 23–24)

A

1 $2a$
2 $3p$
3 $5y$
4 $3f$
5 $5a$
6 $8b$
7 $2g$
8 $7b$
9 $7f$
10 12
11 y
12 $6p$
13 $6e$
14 $5b$
15 $-2y$
16 $3a, 3b$
17 a
18 $4y^2$

B

1 $2p$
2 $8a$
3 $6a$
4 $7b + c$
5 $5a$
6 $2f$
7 $4a + 2b$
8 $4y$
9 0
10 $4a + 3b$
11 $6a + 4b$
12 $4a + 2b$

C

1 $3a$
2 $6x$
3 $7a$
4 $7y$
5 $4a + b$
6 $2y + 3$
7 $2y + 3x$
8 $5a + b$
9 $3x + 3y$
10 $3p + 2q$
11 $7a + 5b$
12 $7y - 3x + 5$
13 $2f + 2g + e$
14 $6x - 3y$
15 $x^2 + 2x$
16 $2p^2 - 2p$

Mixing it up (p. 25)

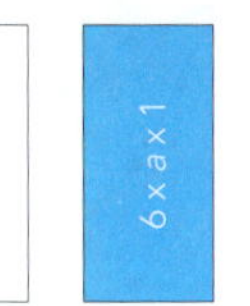

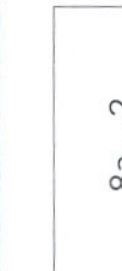

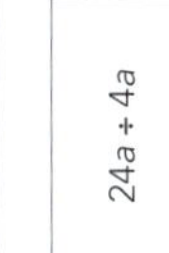

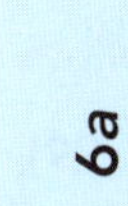

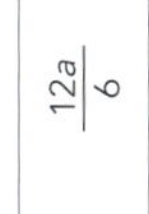

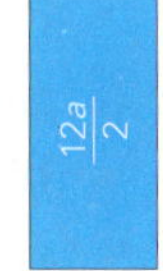

Find the errors (p. 25)

	✓/✗	Correct solution
1	✗	$10t^2$
2	✗	$\frac{4}{m}$
3	✓	
4	✓	
5	✗	$6a + 5$
6	✗	$3p^2$
7	✓	

ISBN: 9780170447416

Powers (pp. 26–33)

Multiplying powers (pp. 17–18)

1	a^2	2	b^5
3	y^3	4	$2f^3$
5	$6p^2$	6	$8d^5$
7	a^4	8	$2ab$
9	b^3	10	a^3
11	y^6	12	m^6
13	$2g^3$	14	$12b^5$
15	$12a^3$	16	$21p^6$
17	$15h^5$	18	b^7
19	$20y^6$	20	h^7
21	$6a^4$	22	a^2b^2
23	$24f^2g^2$	24	$2y^2z^2$
25	y^3z^3	26	$6a^5b^3$
27			

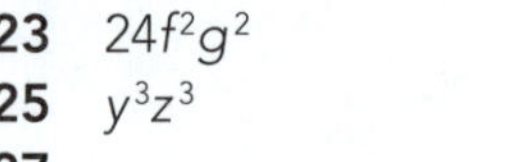

The term left over is $2a$.

Dividing powers (pp. 28–29)

1	b^3	2	f^3
3	$7a^8$	4	$\frac{b^3}{3}$
5	a^2b^2	6	$3f^2g^4$
7	b^4	8	c^3
9	z^2	10	y^5
11	a^4	12	g
13	$3p$	14	$2y$
15	$4b$	16	$4a^3$
17	$\frac{g^2}{3}$	18	yz^2

Find the errors (p. 29)

	✓/✗	Correct solution
1	✗	y^2
2	✗	a^2
3	✓	
4	✓	
5	✗	2
6	✗	xy^2

Powers of powers (pp. 30–31)

1	a^6	2	b^{12}
3	$4f^2$	4	$4y^8$
5	$25g^6$	6	y^6z^4
7	$9x^2y^2$	8	$16a^2b^4$
9	$36g^6h^2$	10	$4y^6z^4$
11	b^{15}	12	a^{32}
13	$4x^6$	14	$27y^{12}$
15	a^6b^2	16	$20p^6$
17	$x^{12}y^4$	18	$4a^2b^2$
19	$16d^{10}e^{20}$	20	$125p^{18}q^3$
21	$9a^2b^4$	22	$8p^6q^{12}$
23			

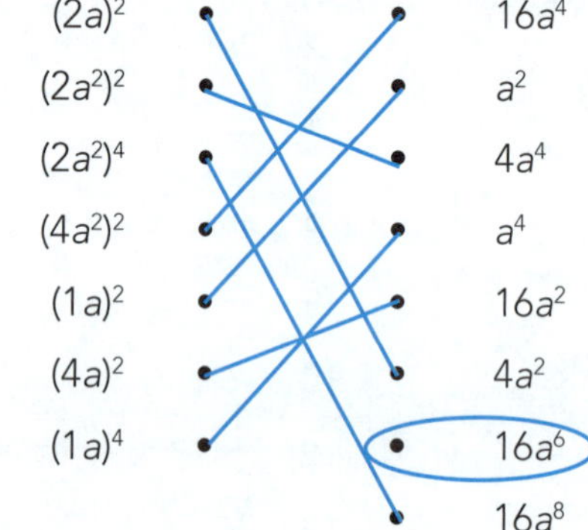

The term left over is $16a^6$.

Mixing it up (p. 32)

A

1	a^6	2	a^{10}
3	b^{12}	4	g^2
5	a^2	6	d^{15}
7	e^5	8	$9f^2$
9	$2y^2$	10	$3a^3$
11	$8k^4$	12	$16p^6$

B

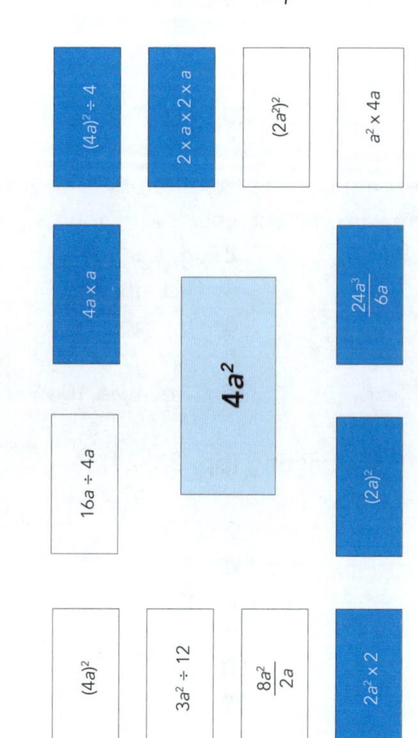

ISBN: 9780170447416

Find the errors (p. 33)

	✓/✗	Explanation	Correct solution
1	✗	There are only four, not five	$4p$
2	✗	You cannot add unlike terms together	$2f^2 + f$
3	✓		
4	✗	Need to multiply the indices	a^6
5	✗	Indices need to be subtracted	$2y$
6	✗	Indices need to be added	$6z^5$
7	✓		
8	✗	5 also needs to be cubed	$125b^3$
9	✓		
10	✓		

Challenge 2 (p. 34)

1

$3a^2 + a + 8a^2$

$12a^2 \div a^4$

$-12a \times -a$

$\frac{12a^3b}{ab}$

$3a^2 \times 4a$

$12a^2$

$\frac{24a^6}{2a^4}$

$\frac{12a^2}{a}$

$(4a)^3$

$3a \times 4$

$20a^2 + 3 - 8a^2$ -3

$-2a \times -6a$

$a + a \times 12$

2

♥ = 4

☺ = 3

✚ = 6

♣ = 8

☾ = 30

Brackets (pp. 35–40)

Expanding (pp. 35–36)

A

1 $2x$ **2** 6
3 $5y$ **4** $6b$
5 $2x$ **6** 15
7 $3y$ **8** $2g$
9 $2x$ **10** $5y$
11 $10a$ **12** 12

B

1 $2a + 2b$ **2** $3x + 6$
3 $5y + 10$ **4** $4a - 8$
5 $2x - 2y$ **6** $xy + xz$
7 $6x + 8$ **8** $x^2 + 3x$

C

1 $2x + 8$ **2** $3x + 12$
3 $5y - 10$ **4** $6x - 24$
5 $2a + 2c$ **6** $3x - 3y$
7 $4x + 6$ **8** $6b - 6$
9 $12 + 4y$ **10** $10 - 2y$
11 $2x + 2y + 2z$ **12** $a^2 + 5a$
13 $6a + 2b + 2c$ **14** $12a + 6ab$

Factorising (pp. 37–40)

A

1 12: 1, 2, 3, **4**, 6, 12
20: 1, 2, **4**, 5, 10, 20
Highest common factor is **4**

2 18: 1, 2, 3, **6**, 9, 18
30: 1, 2, 3, 5, **6**, 15, 30
Highest common factor is **6**

3 24: 1, 2, 4, 6, **12**, 24
36: 1, 2, 3, 4, 6, 9, **12**, 36
Highest common factor is **12**

B

1 1, 2, **4** **2** 1, **2**
3 1, 2, **4** **4** 1, **5**
5 1, 2, 4, **8** **6** 1, **2**
7 1, **2** **8** 1, **3**
9 **1** **10** 1, ***a***
11 1, ***x*** **12** 1, y, 2, ***2y***

C

1 x **2** 1
3 2 **4** 5
5 x **6** 3
7 3 **8** x
9 y **10** 3

D

1 3 **2** 2
3 5 **4** 4
5 4 **6** 2
7 2 **8** 6
9 a **10** x
11 3 **12** 5

ISBN: 9780170447416

E

1 $x + 5$
2 $x + 2$
3 $x + 5$
4 $x - 2$
5 $x - 3$
6 $2x - 3$
7 $2 + x$
8 $4 - x$
9 $f + h$
10 $c - e$
11 $2 - x$
12 $x + 10$

F

1 $2(x + 2)$
2 $6(x + y)$
3 $5(x + 2)$
4 $2(x - 4)$
5 $3(x - 4)$
6 $2(5x + 4)$
7 $4(3 + y)$
8 $3(3 - x)$
9 $6(x - y)$
10 $a(b + c)$

G

1 $3(x + y)$
2 $5(x - y)$
3 $2(x + 4)$
4 $5(x - 2)$
5 $4(x + 3)$
6 $4(x - 6)$
7 $3(2 + x)$
8 $5(3 - x)$
9 $y(x + z)$
10 $2(1 - 3x)$
11 $x(3 + y)$
12 $2y(x + 2z)$
13 $a(4 + b)$
14 $5(1 + 3y)$
15 $y(5x + 6)$
16 $x(y + 1)$
17 $h(1 + g)$
18 $2a(b + 1)$

Challenge 3 (p. 40)

1 $3(2x + 3)$
2 $5(x + y + z)$
3 $x(x + 4)$
4 $2(-x - 5)$ or $-2(x + 5)$
5 $3(-x + 3)$ or $-3(x - 3)$
6 $x(y - z + x)$
7 $2x(x + 2)$
8 $5xz(y - 2)$
9 $x(1 - x)$
10 $y(2x - 4y + x^2)$
11 $x^2(x + 1)$
12 $2x(x - 2 + 4x^2)$

Find the errors (p. 41)

	✓/✗	Correct solution
1	✗	$5d + 20$
2	✓	
3	✗	$6(x + 1)$
4	✓	
5	✗	$10 + 5x$
6	✗	$10(d + f)$
7	✗	$5x + 25$
8	✗	$4(a - 1)$
9	✗	$12(1 - 2x)$
10	✗	$gh - gf$
11	✗	$x(5 - a)$
12	✗	$x(x + 3)$
13	✗	$a(b + c - d)$

Challenge 4 (p. 42)

A

1 $8x + 2y$
2 $-5x - 20$
3 $-3a + 15$
4 $6x + 2xy$
5 $-3x + 6$
6 $5x^2 - 35x$
7 $9x + 21$
8 $5x - 28$

B

1 $xy(2z + 5)$
2 $c(c^2 + 8)$
3 $a(a^3 + 1 - a)$
4 $5pq(5 - 3r)$
5 $x(1 + y - z)$
6 $2k(4k - 2 + 3k^2)$
7 $m^3n^2(m^2 + n^4)$
8 $6g^2(2 + g)$
9 $6(4f - 2f^2 - 5)$
10 $5(3r + 6s - 2t)$

Formulae and substitution (p. 43–46)

With one variable (pp. 43–46)

1 a $L = 22e$
b $L = 22 \times 7$
$= 154$ cm
2 a $T = 35 + 3e$
b $T = 35 + 3 \times 7$
$= 56$ minutes
3 a $A = 12 \times 4$
$= \$48$
b $A = 10h$
c Dairy = \$36
Babysitting = \$40
So babysitting will earn her more money
d \$13 an hour plus \$6 for coming
e $A = 12.50h + 6$
4 a $C = 120 + 3p$
b $C = 120 + 3 \times 35$
$= \$225$
c $C = 150 + 2 \times 35$
$= \$220$
Therefore Battered Buses is cheaper by \$5
d Battered Buses: $C = \$240$
Crummy Coaches: $C = \$255$
e Battered Buses is cheaper by \$15
f Set charge of \$60 plus \$5 per passenger
g Busted Buses: $C = 70 + t + 5s$
5 $N = 13 + 1$
$= 14$
6

Formula	$b = 2$	$b = 4$	$b = 10$	$b = 1$
$A = 2b$	4	8	20	2
$A = b + 5$	7	9	15	6
$A = \frac{20}{b}$	10	5	2	20
$A = 45 - b$	43	41	35	44
$A = b^2$	4	16	100	1
$A = \frac{b + 4}{2}$	3	4	7	2.5

ISBN: 9780170447416

7 a −6 b 5
c −6 d 6
e 4 f 7

Challenge 5 (p. 47)

Formula	$b = 2, c = 2$	$b = 4, c = 1$	$b = 5, c = -1$
$A = b + c$	4	5	4
$A = 4c - b$	6	0	−9
$A = b(c + 2)$	8	12	5
$A = b^2 + c$	6	17	24
$A = 2b^2$	8	32	50
$A = \frac{b+c}{2}$	2	2.5	2
$A = \frac{c+b}{c}$	2	5	−4

Challenge 6 (p. 48)

	[1] 1	[2] 2		[3] 2	5	
[4] 4		8		2		[5] 1
[6] 2	4		[7] 1		[8] 2	7
		[9] 1	4	0		
[10] 1	2		2		[11] 2	[12] 3
3		[13] 1		[14] 1		5
	[15] 4	9		[16] 4	2	

Understanding instructions in algebra (pp. 49–50)

1 Solve ⌘ = 13
2 Simplify $3p + 2f$
3 Expand $2a - 8$
4 Simplify y^2
5 Factorise $3(x + 2)$
6 Evaluate $4 \times 3 + 2 = 14$
7 Expand $9x^4$
8 Solve $b = 5$

Solving linear equations (pp. 51–60)

One-step equations — adding and subtracting (pp. 51–53)

1 $a = 10$ 2 $b = 3$
3 $n = 6$ 4 $u = 6$
5 $y = 16$ 6 $a = 3$
7 $x = 15$ 8 $x = 42$
9 $x = 10$ 10 $x = 20$
11 $y = 24$ 12 $p = 24$
13 $v = 0$ 14 $x = -4$
15 $x = 2$ 16 $y = 3$
17 $h = 18$ 18 $x = 1$
19 $p = 7$ 20 $t = 12$
21 $z = 15$ 22 $x = 9$
23 $y = 10$ 24 $q = 85$
25 $x = -9$ 26 $y = -13$

One-step equations — multiplying and dividing (pp. 54–56)

1 $u = 15$ 2 $f = 10$
3 $n = 4$ 4 $a = 20$
5 $x = 50$ 6 $b = 30$
7 $x = 14$ 8 $x = 6$
9 $x = 8$ 10 $x = 12$
11 $y = 7$ 12 $p = 3$
13 $x = 60$ 14 $x = 28$
15 $y = 3$ 16 $x = -18$
17 $m = 10$ 18 $y = -4$
19 $x = 8$ 20 $g = 3$
21 $x = 4$ 22 $p = 30$
23 $z = 2$ 24 $f = 10$
25 $a = 1$ 26 $q = -4$
27 $d = -2$ 28 $y = -15$

Mixing it up (p. 57)

1 $x = 14$ 2 $a = 6$
3 $x = 19$ 4 $a = 12$
5 $b = 5$ 6 $x = 15$
7 $x = 16$ 8 $y = 15$
9 $a = 7$ 10 $x = 26$
11 $x = 15$ 12 $b = 36$

Find the errors (p. 58)

	✓/✗	Correct solution
1	✗	$x - 6 = 10$ $x = 10 + 6$ $x = 16$
2	✗	$6x = 18$ $x = \frac{18}{6}$ $x = 3$
3	✓	
4	✗	$x + 3 = 8$ $x = 8 - 3$ $x = 5$
5	✓	
6	✗	$\frac{x}{2} = 17$ $x = 17 \times 2$ $x = 34$

ISBN: 9780170447416

Mixing it up (p. 59)

[1]	[1] 2	[2] 1		[3] 1	0	
[4] 3		8		6		[5] 2
[6] 2	4		[7] 2		[8] 1	1
		[9] 1	0	0		
[10] 2	2		1		[11] 1	[12] 2
5		[13] 4		[14] 5		3
	[15] 7	1		[16] 1	3	

Forming then solving linear equations (p. 60)

1 $4x = 20$ $x = 5$
2 $x \div 3 = 5$ $x = 15$
3 $x + 5 = 8$ $x = 3$
4 $x - 2 = 12$ $x = 14$
5 $x \div 3 = 10$ $x = 30$
6 $6x = 12$ $x = 2$
7 $2x = 14$ $x = 7$
8 $x \div 2 = 8$ $x = 16$
9 $x - 3 = 9$ $x = 12$
10 $x + 4 = 6$ $x = 2$

Challenge 7 (p. 61)

1 $x = 2.5$
2 $x = -6$
3 $x = 7$
4 $x = -18$
5 $x = 7$
6 $x = 300$
7 $x = 24$
8 $x = \frac{1}{3}$

Two-step equations (pp. 62–63)

1 $x = 5$
2 $a = 3$
3 $y = 3$
4 $z = 6$
5 $p = 2$
6 $d = 2$
7 $b = 6$
8 $x = 3$
9 $t = 4$
10 $g = 8$
11 $a = 4$
12 $x = 2$
13 $p = 2$
14 $y = 4$
15 $x = 5$
16 $g = 5$
17 $a = 5$
18 $x = 3$

Find the errors (p. 64)

	✓/✗	Correct solution
1	✗	$2g + 2 = 14$ $2g = 14 - 2$ $g = \frac{12}{2}$ $g = 6$
2	✓	
3	✓	
4	✗	$6x - 2 = 10$ $6x = 12$ $x = \frac{12}{6}$ $x = 2$
5	✓	
6	✗	$5y - 3 = 2$ $5y = 2 + 3$ $y = 5 \div 5$ $y = 1$

Forming then solving two-step linear equations (p. 65)

1 $2x - 3 = 7$ $x = 5$
2 $3x + 1 = 10$ $x = 3$
3 $4x + 2 = 18$ $x = 4$
4 $3x - 3 = 6$ $x = 3$
5 $2x + 4 = 10$ $x = 3$
6 $3x - 2 = 1$ $x = 1$
7 $50 + 12w = 182$ $w = 11$
11 weeks
8 $2.25a + 1.50 = 15$ $a = 6$
6 avocados
9 $3x + x = 16$ $x = 4$
Small group is 4, large group is 12
10 $2x + 5 = 31$ $x = 13$

Challenge 8 (p. 66)

1 $y = 5$
2 $x = 18$
3 $x = -2$
4 $x = 6$
5 $x = 4.5$
6 $x = 8$
7 $x = 1$
8 $x = 17$

With variables on both sides (pp. 67–68)

1 $x = 6$
2 $y = 2$
3 $x = 6$
4 $a = 4$
5 $b = 4$
6 $y = 5$
7 $a = 3$
8 $a = 6$
9 $g = 3$
10 $c = 10$
11 $p = 5$
12 $y = 3$
13 $x = 2$
14 $f = 4$
15 $x = 5$
16 $x = -4$

ISBN: 9780170447416

Find the errors (p. 69)

	✓/✗	Correct solution
1	✗	$5a = 12 + a$ $4a = 12$ $a = \frac{12}{4}$ $a = 3$
2	✗	$3p - 6 = p$ $2p = 6$ $p = \frac{6}{2}$ $p = 3$
3	✓	
4	✗	$2x - 1 = 8 - x$ $3x - 1 = 8$ $3x = 9$ $x = 3$
5	✓	
6	✗	$2 + 4z = 2z + 6$ $4z = 2z + 4$ $2z = 4$ $z = \frac{4}{2}$ $z = 2$

With brackets (pp. 70–71)

1 $x = 6$
2 $x = 6$
3 $x = 1$
4 $x = 10$
5 $x = 3$
6 $x = 5$
7 $x = 7$
8 $x = 8$
9 $x = 1$
10 $x = 5$
11 $x = 4$
12 $x = 12$

Find the errors (p. 72)

	✓/✗	Correct solution
1	✓	
2	✗	$5(x + 5) = 25$ $5x + 25 = 25$ $5x = 0$ $x = 0$
3	✓	
4	✗	$2(x + 3) = 12$ $2x + 6 = 12$ $2x = 6$ $x = \frac{6}{2}$ $x = 3$
5	✓	
6	✓	

Mixing it up (p. 73)

	[1] 1	[2] 2		[3] 1	1	
[4] 2		1		5		[5] 2
[6] 1	7		[7] 2		[8] 1	0
		[9] 1	0	4		
[10] 1	5		6		[11] 1	[12] 2
0		[13] 1		[14] 2		2
	[15] 2	3		[16] 2	6	

Challenge 9 (p. 74)

1 $x = 14$
2 $x = 45$
3 $b = 15$
4 $a = 3$
5 $p = 2.5$
6 $y = -6$
7 $x = 7$ cm
8 $x = 15$ cm

Understanding instructions in algebra (pp. 75–76)

1 Solve $x = 3$
2 Simplify $7p + 3q$
3 Factorise $2(x + 6)$
4 Simplify $4y$
5 Expand $3x - 6$
6 Evaluate 3
7 Simplify (or expand) a^8
8 Simplify $6p^2$

ISBN: 9780170447416

Revision 1 (pp. 77–79)

1 $y - 4$

2 Three plus a number

3 a The variable is **w** and it stands for **the number of weeks**.

b \$104

4 a $2p^2$ b $\frac{5}{y}$

c $4g + h$ d $2e + 3f$

e $6y^2$ f a^2b^2

g $25g^6$ h $4z$

5 a $3y + 6$ b $12 - 2x$

6 a $7(p + 2)$ b $2t(t + 3)$

7

Formula	$d = 3$	$d = 6$	$d = 1$	$d = 0$
$A = 32 - d$	29	26	31	32

8 a \$30.50

b Jenny \$27, Mona \$34

Jenny spends less money

c $20 + 3.50r = 34$

$r = 4$

She would need to ride more than four times to make the most of her money

9 a $p = 13$ b $p = 6$

c $f = 5$ d $y = 4$

e $x = 8$ f $x = 7$

10 a $2x = 12$, $x = 6$ b $x - 5 = 9$, $x = 14$

c $2x + 2 = 8$, $x = 3$ d $3x - 2 = 16$, $x = 6$

11 a Expand $2p - 8$

b Evaluate 12

c Solve $x = 9$

d Factorise $2(p + 8)$

Revision 2 (pp. 80–82)

1 $y + 7$

2 Two divided by a number

3 a The variable is **a** and it stands for **the number of animals**.

b 26 minutes

4 a $8y$ b $\frac{p}{5}$

c $3p + 3g$ d $2a + 2b$

e $20mp$ f c^3d

g $8b^6$ h $7y^2$

5 a $2x - 6$ b $mp + np$

6 a $3(x + 4)$ b $x(y + z)$

7

Formula	$d = 2$	$d = 4$	$d = 32$	$d = 0$
$A = \frac{d}{2}$	1	2	16	0

8 a \$65

b Neighbour jobs \$104, dog walking \$112

Walking the dog will earn him more money

9 a $y = 8$ b $p = 28$

c $b = 7$ d $a = 5$

e $y = 4$ f $x = 11$

10 a $x \div 2 = 9$, $x = 18$ b $x + 3 = 10$, $x = 7$

c $2x + 2 = 6$, $x = 2$ d $4x - 3 = 9$, $x = 3$

11 a Simplify $p + 4r$

b Simplify (or expand) $4y^2$

c Expand $4x + 12$

d Solve $x = 5$

ISBN: 9780170447416